Getting Ahead as an
International Student

Getting Ahead as an International Student

Dave Burnapp

Open University Press

Open University Press
McGraw-Hill Education
McGraw-Hill House
Shoppenhangers Road
Maidenhead
Berkshire
England
SL6 2QL

email: enquiries@openup.co.uk
world wide web: www.openup.co.uk

and Two Penn Plaza, New York, NY 10121-2289, USA

First published 2009, Reprinted 2011

A catalogue record of this book is available from the British Library

ISBN-13: 978-0-33-523453-0 (pb)   978-0-33-523452-3 (hb)
ISBN-10: 0-335-23453-4 (pb)   0-335-23452-6 (hb)

Library of Congress Cataloging-in-Publication Data
CIP data applied for

Typeset by RefineCatch Limited, Bungay, Suffolk
Printed in the UK by CPI Antony Rowe, Chippenham, Wiltshire.

The *McGraw·Hill* Companies

Contents

Introduction

Aims of this book

This book has been written for international students who are planning to study at a university in an English speaking country, for example the UK, Australia, Ireland, the USA and New Zealand. There are small differences between the universities in these countries, and indeed differences between universities within each of these countries – and even between two **faculties** within a single university. Despite this, these institutions share certain beliefs about what knowledge is, and thence what activities students and teachers should undertake.

For the remainder of this book all mentions of 'university' should be taken to refer to 'universities in English speaking countries' and it is accepted that in other countries universities have very different approaches, and indeed that is one reason why this book is necessary. Please also note that words in bold, for example '**faculties**', are defined in the **Glossary** at the end of the book.

As a result of engaging with this book you will develop a clear idea of university life and student life styles, but above all you will have a clear idea of the language skills, study skills and communication skills which are necessary at university. Many books aimed at international students can make the same claim, but this book goes further: instead of just teaching you what is expected (for example explaining that you are expected to participate in **seminars**, or that you are expected to give exact **references** to your sources), this book helps you to explore the theories held in these universities about what knowledge is, and then shows you how the expected behaviours of teachers and students arise from these theories. For example you are expected to participate in seminars because of a deeply held belief that knowledge comes about from discussion, a theory concerning the **social construction** of knowledge. This book is original because it sets out to help you understand *why* you will be asked to do certain things, as well as covering *what* you will be asked to do and *how* to do them.

Throughout this book you will be asked to compare the methods and approaches in these universities with your previous experiences, not because you have to forget your previous methods and approaches, but because of another theory, known as **reflective learning**, which sees learning as a process of change and development. You will also read the words of other international students reflecting on their own experiences.

Who should use this book

This book is suitable for any students who intend to attend one of these universities to do a **degree** course of any kind, including **undergraduate**, **postgraduate**, **top-up**, **exchange** programmes, or **distance learning** programmes. This book will be of most use for students of humanities and social sciences, in particular in business schools, as it does not cover the specific requirements of the hard sciences and engineering. You may use this book as a part of some kind of preparation programme, for example **pre-departure courses**, **induction** courses, or **International Foundation Programmes**. In this case as well as finding out about the culture of these universities you will be able to use the many tasks in the book to put into practice the methods described, working sometimes on your own, at other times in pairs or in small groups. As a result when you begin your degree course you will have had lots of practice in the necessary skills. Other students may use this book working individually to prepare for university – in this case you need to get some friends to discuss some of the tasks with. In order to get maximum benefit from this book you must find situations where you are with people who have different experiences and different ideas in order to use and to hear the most important phrase in these universities: 'In my opinion . . .'

The structure of this book

Part One: The university context

The four chapters in this part of the book will help you to understand what universities in English speaking countries are like. There are, of course, enormous differences between all these institutions; some are historic with traditions going back hundreds of years, while others are much more modern and concentrate on developing high-tech facilities. Some universities are in city centres, and indeed can sometimes be the most important buildings in the city; others are set on a **campus**, similar to a park, somewhere out of town.

All of them, however, share certain features – a culture of learning, a way of behaving, a set of beliefs and values – which are the focus of the first part of this book. Although the main aim is to describe this culture, you will also do lots of activities such as readings and discussions which themselves are an introduction to some of the methods that you will explore more deeply later in the book. In every chapter there are several learning tips which give direct and practical suggestions to help you with your studies, and in Chapter 3 there are some living tips, as you will not be studying all the time, to help you to lead a balanced life. Most importantly there are a series of tasks for you to keep in your course **portfolio** which will be described later in this introduction. Completing the portfolio is the best way to ensure that you prepare yourself for your university course.

The four chapters in Part One are:

1 What are English speaking universities like?
2 What sort of changes will I need to make?
3 What sort of things will I have to do?
4 What sort of **assessments** will I have?

Part Two: The study process

In this part of the book you will explore the methods of studying which are commonly used in English speaking universities, to see what people in these universities believe knowledge actually is, and the things you will be expected to do as a student. It is important that you really understand these requirements, so the activities here will help you to understand why certain things are expected as well as showing you how to do the required study tasks. This part of the book will take you through the stages that students follow each time they begin a new **module** or a new area of study.

The four chapters in this Part are:

5 Starting out: what do I already know?
6 How can I understand my topic?
7 How do these ideas connect?
8 Group working: what do other people think?

Part Three: Producing assignments

There are many different types of assessment used in universities, and the three chapters in Part Three of the book will take you through the stages which you should follow to produce **assignments**, which demonstrate your learning. This involves a change from **extensive** studying techniques, when you get broad general ideas, to more **intensive** techniques, when you go more deeply into specific issues and follow the exact requirements demanded in your assignment instructions.

The three chapters in this Part are:

9 What do I have to do to excel in my assessments?
10 What is **critical awareness** and how can I show it in my work?
11 Finishing off, have I done what was required?

The methods used in this book

Each chapter begins with an introductory exercise which asks you to think about the ideas you have on a topic, and then the topics are presented as a series of explanations with accompanying tasks so you can try out the methods and skills being presented. These tasks will involve reading a variety of texts, taking part in discussions, reflecting on your own experiences, and doing some writing exercises in different styles. In Parts Two and Three you will learn about the process of studying a new topic, and the process of producing assignments, and each chapter in these two Parts is structured into three sections: approaches, methods and skills.

- **Approaches:** these outline the theories of learning and teaching associated with this stage of the learning process.
- **Methods:** these will describe the particular behaviours of students and teachers which arise from these approaches.
- **Skills:** these are exercises to develop the study skills (including language and personal skills) necessary for these methods.

The learning portfolio

You should keep copies of many of the tasks in a portfolio. The word 'portfolio' really means a kind of folder which is used to keep different pieces of paper, and portfolios are now often used in assessments, which means that throughout a course you keep adding things as you progress. At the end of the course your portfolio will contain lots of different items (exercises, notes, **case studies**, etc.) that you have added. Some courses may use **e-portfolios**, where you save your materials online.

You should divide your portfolio into two parts. Part A of your portfolio is 'the learning log'. This is like a diary: it will contain reflective writing about your feelings about different tasks in the course. For example you will sometimes work in groups to research or to make **presentations**. This process (searching for information, working as a group, preparing and delivering a presentation) will always involve some difficulties, some new activities and some things you feel proud that you have achieved. These are the kinds of experiences you should describe in your learning log. Part B of the portfolio is about 'application activities'. For example you will sometimes need to complete worksheets or exercises. For these you will make a larger copy of the worksheets to give yourself plenty of room to write in. You will find out more about how to keep a portfolio in Chapter 5 of this book.

Employability

You will see that the types of learning you will use during a degree are all linked to developing skills which will help you in your future career. Each chapter in Parts Two and Three of this book therefore has a section which illustrates how the approaches, methods and skills presented in that chapter can be applied in employment.

Critical incidents

The aim of this book is to prepare you to operate in a new culture. A common method of training for crossing cultures, for example for staff working in multinational companies, is in discussing **critical incidents**. These are descriptions of situations involving people from different cultures where something has gone wrong, and through discussing the expectations of the different people involved it is possible to gain insight into how inappropriate behaviours have resulted from cultural differences. Each chapter in Parts Two and Three therefore concludes with one such critical incident for discussion and reflection.

Here is an example:

A teacher at a UK university had invited a group of international students to go to the cinema. The group decided to use two cars, and to meet outside the cinema at 6.30pm to buy the tickets for a showing of the film at around 8pm, and then to go to eat together while waiting for the time of the film. The teacher and half of the students arrived on time in one car, but then a student in the second car rang to say that they were still waiting for one student to arrive. By the time the second car arrived it was after 7 o'clock. The student who caused the lateness did not apologize and several of the students seemed to think it was a joke, they laughed and said that the same student was always late for everything. The teacher was obviously angry, but none of the students seemed to be angry at the time. Later one of the students told the teacher, in private, that some of the students thought less of him because he had shown that he was angry.

1   To what extent do you agree or disagree with the teacher / the student who was late / the other students?
2   If you were the teacher / the student who was late / the other students what would you have done?
3   Why do you think the student who was late / the other students behaved as they did?
4   Why do you think the teacher felt as he did?

Intended learning outcomes

On successful completion of the tasks in this book students will be able to:

- Identify different cultures of learning and learning styles related to university level studying.
- Differentiate techniques of **constructivist** learning, reflective learning and **autonomous** learning in course requirements.
- Demonstrate high level learning skills: **analysis**, **synthesis**, **evaluation** and critical awareness in assessed course work.
- Employ a range of researching skills and appropriate reading strategies, utilizing appropriate note-taking strategies in preparing coursework.
- Differentiate **declarative knowledge** and **functional knowledge** required in assignment instructions.
- Assess the suitability of different source texts (for example online and mass-media) in autonomous study.
- Construct a connected argument, correctly incorporating information from sources into the students' own writing.
- Employ basic **primary research**: **quantitative** (survey design) and **qualitative** (interview schedules) in project work.

Key skills

Communication

- Participate in discussions in pairs, small groups and project groups.
- Distinguish between **subjective** and **objective** writing styles, selecting when each is appropriate.

Application of number

- Present findings from quantitative research graphically in coursework.

Information technology

- Use online search engines to locate web based information.
- Use PowerPoint to deliver effective oral presentations.

Working with others

- Assess reasons for volunteering and types of volunteering.
- Demonstrate team working skills.
- Give and receive **feedback** on performance.

Improving own learning and performance

- Create links between studying and employment skills.
- Examine own preferred learning styles.
- Create time management plans for their own learning and for independent living.
- Present information orally and in writing at professional standards.

Problem solving

- Make an action plan concerning life changes.

Part One

The university context

Introduction

The four chapters here will help you to understand what universities in English speaking countries are like. As you go through each chapter you need to complete the tasks and keep some of these in your course portfolio which was outlined in the Introduction to this book. Completing the portfolio is the best way for you to prepare yourself for going to university.

The four chapters in Part One are:

1 What are English speaking universities like?
2 What sort of changes will I need to make?
3 What sort of things will I have to do?
4 What sort of assessments will I have?

1

What are English speaking universities like?

Theme: Maslow's hierarchy of needs

> **Aims of this chapter**
>
> By the end of this chapter you will have:
>
> - Examined your expectations concerning forthcoming changes in your life.
> - Learnt about one theory concerning human motivation.
> - Reviewed some research about adaptation of international students.
> - Found out about types of student accommodation and eating.
> - Seen the link between studying and employment.
> - Discovered some of the forms of support available to you at English speaking universities.
> - Made an action plan concerning settling in to living in your new university.

Introductory exercise: life changes

When people leave home to go to live in another country they can find the experience is both exciting and rewarding, but it may also bring changes which can sometimes make them feel anxious. Think of your own situation: you are either planning to study abroad or have already moved to a new situation where you are an international student.

Task 1.1   Examining your own expectations

Number the factors in the following list from 1 to 10, where 1 is the item that makes you feel the most anxious; 2, the second most anxious; and so on.

- Leaving friends and family.
- Eating different food.
- Living in a strange town.
- Making new friends.
- Using a foreign language.
- Finding a place to live.
- Finding a part time job.
- Dealing with officials (for example visa officers, bank administrators, etc.)
- Living in a different climate.
- Being alone.

Are there any further anxieties you want to add?

Task 1.2   Discussion in pairs

If you are doing this course with a group of other students, then compare your list from the task above with a classmate, on the other hand if you are following this course alone then show your list to a friend. Together discuss how people can deal with these life changes. Remember that the step you are taking (going to live and study in another country) is something which can be stressful for anybody, even if most of the experience will be positive and enriching.

Learning tip   Try to get into the habit of opening up your feelings like this, of discussing your experiences with others, because you will see later, in Chapter 5, that this type of reflection is sometimes expected in university assignments.

Why begin by discussing support?

Although most of this book will explain and help you to practise the skills you will need for studying, in this chapter you will find out about other aspects of student life, such as where you will live and what you will eat. All universities provide plenty of support for all of their students, on topics such as health, accommodation, adaptation and so on, so this chapter introduces you to some of the services which universities provide to support students in these areas. The following activity will examine one very influential theory to explain why we are first discussing these topics.

Online reading: Maslow's hierarchy of needs

On the website connected to this book www.openup.co.uk/international students there are three readings which refer to this theory:

1   Santrock, J. W. (2004) *Educational Psychology*, 2nd edn. Maidenhead: McGraw-Hill. (Extract '*Perspectives on Motivation*', pp. 415–17).
2   Times100 (2005) *Motivation*. Online. MBA Publishing Ltd, Tadcaster. © The Times Newspapers Ltd and MBA Publishing Ltd 1995–2008.
3   Wirral Metropolitan College (n.d.) *Motivation: Introduction to First Line Management*. Online. Wirral Metropolitan College, Birkenhead. Copyright © Wirral Metropolitan College.

Task 1.3   Online reading

Read through the above three source texts online then look at the following student's summary:

Maslow's hierarchy of needs

This theory, which was developed over many years by Abraham Maslow, originated in the field of psychology but it is influential in a range of other areas including education (Santrock 2004) and management (Times100 2005; Wirral Metropolitan College n.d.). A key element of this theory is the idea that people have rising levels of need, so they can only try to satisfy their higher needs when their more basic needs have already been satisfied. This is important for managers because they must understand what motivates the workers in their organisation: 'True motivation is achieved by fulfilling higher order needs' (Times100 2005). In education this is just one of many different psychological theories which are used to examine students' motivation. In order to demonstrate Maslow's theory in its most simple way, Santrock (2004) points out that if students are hungry they are unlikely to be able to do their best.

Maslow's levels are usually presented as a pyramid (see Figure 1.1), and a range of terms are used to describe the different levels. At the bottom of the pyramid are physiological needs: what a body needs to survive such as food, water and somewhere to sleep. The next level is for safety or security: this includes the protection of family and society; in the workplace, it relates to safety issues that managers should bear in mind when considering their workers' motivation (Times100 2005). The next level relates to group or social needs: this includes a sense of belonging, or love; and, in education, this relates to a student's need to feel they are noticed and included in groups. The fourth level is esteem, which concerns respect: both your own feeling of self-esteem

---

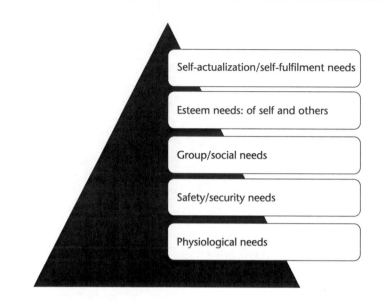

Self-actualization/self-fulfilment needs

Esteem needs: of self and others

Group/social needs

Safety/security needs

Physiological needs

Figure 1.1   Maslow's hierarchy of needs

and recognition of other people's needs for esteem. The highest level refers to self-actualization needs or self-fulfilment needs: 'concerned with full personal development and individual creativity' (Times100 2005). Getting a university degree is at this highest level of self-fulfilment. It should be remembered that Maslow's theory is only one theory among many and, although very influential, it has been criticized and amended by other psychologists.

References

Santrock, J. W. (2004) *Educational Psychology*, 2nd edn. Maidenhead: McGraw-Hill.

Times100 (2005) *Motivation*. Online. Tadcaster: MBA Publishing Ltd. Available at: http://www.thetimes100.co.uk/downloads/theory/motivation.pdf (accessed 21 April 2008).

Wirral Metropolitan College (n.d.) *Motivation: Introduction to First Line Management*. Online. Birkenhead: Wirral Metropolitan College. Available at: http://www.wmc.ac.uk/flm/motivation/maslow.html (accessed 21 April 2008).

Research into international students' adaptation

Recently an organization concerned with international students in the UK carried out research into their experiences in all areas of their life. This is a quotation from the report which uses Maslow's theory to explain its findings about students' adaptation:

> Maslow's (1970) hierarchy of needs suggests that human beings' physiological needs (such as food and housing) and 'safety' (a stable, predictable environment), must be met before they can focus on higher level needs such as self-development. This indicates why students need to be confident about meeting their basic needs of finance and accommodation and feeling secure within the unfamiliar environment of their place of study, before they can concentrate on their studies.
>
> (UKCOSA 2004: 31)

Learning tip UKCISA (the new name for UKCOSA) is an advisory body which gives advice and assistance to international students and to colleges and universities in the UK who recruit international students. It is a very good idea to go to the UKCISA website for guidance on all aspects of being an international student in the UK. For example you can download fact sheets concerning accommodation, finance and visas at: http://www.ukcosa.org.uk/

If you are thinking of going to Australia then look for information and advice on the website of IDP at: http://www.idp.com/

Task 1.4 Applying Maslow's theory

Here are ten comments made by a group of new international students just a few days after they arrived at a university in the UK. They were asked to identify:

What questions do you want answers to?

Their answers included:

1 How long does it generally take for an international student to find a part time job?
2 Where can I find fast food at reasonable prices?

What is your most important need?

Their answers included:

3 A good group of friends and a shared hostel room at cheap rates.
4 An electric adaptor as my computer cannot plug in here.

What is your biggest surprise?

Their answers included:

5   There is no arrangement for food along with the accommodation for people living in halls.
6   Difficulty in finding accommodation.

What is your biggest achievement since arriving?

Their answers included:

7   Made some good friends and cooked food for the first time without burning it (surprising!).
8   I am pleased with what I have done with my room: I have arranged everything in good order in a tiny room.

What advice would you give to students planning to come to the UK?

Their answers included:

9   Learn cooking, and what to carry and what not to carry in baggage.
10   The most important thing is to improve their English.

Can you match each of these students' answers with the five levels taken from Maslow? Put your answers in Part B of your portfolio.

Self-actualization/Self-fulfilment needs:	
Esteem needs: self and others:	
Group/social needs:	
Safety/security needs:	
Physiological needs:	

Task 1.5   Small group discussion

If you are doing this course with a group of other students then compare your answers with classmates, and if you are following this course alone then show your list to a friend. Do you agree that it is necessary for students to deal with issues such as food, accommodation and friendship before it is possible to concentrate on their studies? What things do you think you will need to arrange before you can settle down to studying properly?

Support services

The UKCOSA report investigated a range of topics related to adaptation, but here we will focus of three topics only: accommodation (including food); careers services; and the various guidance schemes available in most universities.

Accommodation

Three female postgraduate students (one from Nigeria, one from India and one from China) are now living in the same university **hall of residence**. Their flat is for females only, but some other flats on their campus are mixed, with males and females sharing. The university is quite new; it is on a campus which is like a large park with lots of trees and grass. In the hall where these students live there are eight people in each flat, every student has their own bedroom, and there is a shared kitchen in every flat. The hall is self-catering, which means the students need to shop and cook for themselves. Each bedroom in these students' flat has its own en suite shower and toilet, but some other flats nearby have shared toilets and showers.

A few days after arriving at the university these students were chatting about the types of accommodation they had experienced previously. Here is part of that discussion:

> *Ronke:* When I was in Nigeria I studied in different parts of the country, so there were some differences because Nigeria is a big country with different cultures. The universities usually had different hostels for boys and girls, and in some places the boys could visit the girls' hostels in the daytime and evenings, but in other places this wasn't allowed. There were lots of hostels, so getting a place usually wasn't difficult. A big difference between home and the UK is that here the facilities in the students' accommodation are all working, but in some hostels at home there was not a lot of maintenance. I've also heard that in my old university they are planning to put in bunk beds, so soon there will be eight people in each room whereas there were only four in each room when I stayed there. The equipment in the hostel was basic, so you had to bring your own fan and fridge if you could afford it. Here in England most students have got their own single room, with their own table and so on. The hostels in Nigeria are bigger and more crowded, usually four floors with eighty students in each corridor. In the rooms there were just a couple of wardrobes

and cupboards, and two tables for studying. There were various restaurants with food at different prices, so really food was not an issue; you had to pay for your food each time you went to the restaurant, and some people would cook food on camping gas cookers in the corridors. I usually used to eat out most days.

Kiran: Yes, I had different experiences in India too, at different colleges. I went to one college which was only for girls, and there we were 200 girls together in our hostel, all like one big family: we ate together, and watched TV in a common room together. Here in the UK there seems to be a lot more privacy, but perhaps that can also mean people are sometimes more lonely, I don't know. Boys were never allowed to come into the hostel in India; they couldn't even come into the gate! I was surprised when I first learnt that some of the student halls in the UK are mixed. Because India is so diverse we had different kinds of food, vegetarian and non-vegetarian, but there would never be beef or pork. The food was nutritious but perhaps not too tasty. It was possible to prepare your own snacks also, but you didn't have to cook your own meals the way we do here in England. We paid for the accommodation and the food all together as a package, so we did not have to pay for each meal. I think the English system of self-catering is more like what we call 'paying guests' in India, that is when students rent a place near the university, then they can have their own room and do their own cooking, in fact some even employ their own maid and cook.

Yuan: In my university in China you paid for each meal each time you ate, and there were lots of different restaurants around the campus, and different styles of food, for example people from some regions liked certain styles of cooking. You were not allowed to cook in your rooms, but it wasn't necessary as there are so many restaurants and the food is not expensive. For the accommodation in my university all the students had to live on the campus, which was a rule. The boys and the girls were separate, and the boys could not come into the girls' hostels, or could just come to the ground floor but could not go upstairs. In my university there were eight students in each room, so the room was quite crowded. You had to share bathrooms, but here in the UK some students have their own single bedroom with their own bathroom and toilet, that is very good. One thing I miss here concerns sports facilities, in China all universities have lots of sports facilities all around the campus: table tennis, badminton, volley ball and basket ball, we usually played a quick game between lessons and I think that is good for studying.

Task 1.6   Portfolio task

Our expectations about the future are strongly influenced by our previous experience, and this is true for all of us. When you read information about accommodation for students in another country you will certainly interpret it using your own previous experiences of student accommodation. If, however, you bring your assumptions into the open you may be able to see differences more clearly. For this writing task you should describe your own experiences of student accommodation in your own country: how many people shared the room; how was food prepared; were there any rules you had to follow; were there problems of loneliness; how expensive was it? If you lived at home, describe what you think is typical accommodation for students in your country. Write around 200 words, and put this into Part A of your portfolio.

Types of university accommodation

Not all universities in the UK are campus universities, for example some have buildings scattered around city centres. Not all university halls of residence are self-catering, in some there are dining rooms with meals prepared at set times. Not all students live in university supplied accommodation, some live with their families, and many rent houses away from the university which they share with other students. In big cities there are also student halls run by private companies. However, almost every university will have an accommodation service which will help you to find a place to live.

Learning tip   If you know which university you are going to study at then look at its website and find out about the accommodation they offer, do not assume it will be like the accommodation you are used to, or even like the accommodation of other people you may know who already are studying in the same country.

Task 1.7   Reading

Look at this information leaflet which one university sends to international students: it talks about making choices, so as you read it think about the choices you would make if you were going to this university.

University Accommodation Offices: Accommodation for international students

You have the choice of either living on campus in one of the university Halls of Residence or living in a private rented house.
Halls of Residence: these are popular with first year students and international students in particular. Living on campus is a good way to

meet new friends and you are also close to all the university facilities (both the library for studying and the **Students' Union** for parties and music). Also you don't need to worry about things like electricity bills because everything is included in your rent. We also have some halls which are reserved especially for postgraduate students, and many of our rooms have constant broadband Internet access. On the campus there are many different types of rooms, but all of our halls are self catering and you will find that the campus supermarket sells most of the things you will need (also see below for information about restaurants on the campus). The choices you need to make are:

- Do you want a single room or a double room? (Single rooms are more expensive).
- Do you want en suite or shared bathrooms? (En suite rooms are more expensive).
- Do you want a room with or without Internet connection? (Internet connected rooms are more expensive).
- Do you want a Hall near the town centre or in the Park Campus? (The prices are similar).

Private sector: many students prefer to live away from the university and to share a house with other students, but our accommodation office can still help you, as we want to be sure that you find a safe place to live. We keep a database of private landlords whose properties are of acceptable standards. To check they are acceptable, we inspect them once every year. On our database we have a large number of houses, many within a mile of the university and others in the town centre, usually suitable for four students to share. This can be cheaper than rooms on campus, but you will also have to pay electricity bills and perhaps pay for transport to the university each day.

Restaurants on campus

- The main students' refectory is open every day from 8.00 to 20.00, and this has a full range of hot and cold meals.
- The Student's Union has a snack bar which serves fast food from 12.00 until 22.00. There are also two bars in the Student's Union which sell sandwiches at lunchtime.
- The Lake Restaurant is open from 12.00–14.00, and from 18.00–22.00 for more formal dining.
- There is also a coffee bar connected to the library which has dispensing machines which are available 24 hours.

Task 1.8   Portfolio task

What questions do you want answers to concerning food and accommodation? Write ten questions concerning food and accommodation that you need answers to: be practical, think of things like cost, location, facilities, regulations and so on. One topic discovered in the UKCOSA research mentioned earlier is that in some universities it is necessary to move out of campus accommodation during university holidays (and move out all of your belongings). Would that be a difficulty for you? Put this list of questions into Part B of your portfolio.

Careers services

Task 1.9   Preparing for employment

You may think that it will not be necessary to find out about the university **careers service** until you are near the end of your course, but one careers advisor, who works at a university in central England, suggests you should make contact with the careers service as early as you can. This is an extract from a talk she gave to new students. Read what she has to say, and then do the exercise below.

It is really important to begin preparing for employment from the very beginning of your stay. It is true that there are various schemes which allow international students to work after they graduate so they can get experience which will help them find work when they go home, but there is a lot of competition to get these jobs. You need to begin finding out as soon as you can about how the labour market operates here, and that is one way the careers service can help you; we arrange practical help such as how to prepare applications and a *CV*, how to make online applications, and we run sessions to practise for interviews. We also have many events each year where students can meet employers and find out what they need.

While you are still studying there are a lot of things you can begin to do to improve your chances of finding a good job later, for example the careers service can give you information about finding part-time work, which can be very useful because apart from earning some money this also introduces you to the way that companies here operate. You might only be stacking shelves in a supermarket in your part-time job and that can sometimes be boring, but you will still need to fill out an application form and to be interviewed, you will have staff training at different times, and you will have to sign a contract; all of these are things which are typical of this culture of work.

There are also some **volunteering** schemes which can be useful, so if you want to work in education then volunteering to help in a school homework club will give you experience of working with children, and this will be valuable for you later. Volunteers, of course, are not paid.

Another area which is becoming more important involves some form of **work placement** – some people call this internship – where you work for a few months in a company during a holiday, and in fact some students do this for a full year and complete assignments and get **credits** towards their degree. This will mean that your course will take one extra year. You must remember that university education really is about developing knowledge and skills which are needed in the workplace.

What are the advantages and disadvantages of the different types of employment she mentioned, also add your own ideas: what do you think about these types of employment?

Type of work	Advantages	Disadvantages
Part time work		
Volunteering		
Work placements		
Work experience after graduating		

Guidance

You saw at the beginning of this chapter that the life changes involved in going to live and study in another country can at times cause some anxiety. All universities have a lot of **support services** which are used by all students. Here we look at this support in two ways: if you have a question; and if you want to talk.

If you have question

Probably many other students before you have asked the same question that you need an answer to, so expect that the information you are looking for is already available; on a website, in a leaflet, or on a notice board. Look at the following learning tips:

Learning tip   Make sure you attend all the induction sessions for new students at the beginning of your studies – this is when a lot of information is given out.

Learning tip   Get to know your university facilities: explore the university, go into the different departments such as student services buildings, the library, and the health centre and look around.

Learning tip   Look at notice boards around the university, pick up and read leaflets you find.

Learning tip   Get to know the university website, click on the links and use the 'search' facility to find out about the services; use the search box to search for 'health', 'library', 'bookshop', or 'timetable'.

If you want to talk

There may be times when you want someone to talk to, not to solve your problems for you but to listen to you. Most universities have the following services/schemes:

- *Clubs and societies.* 'Prevention is better than cure', so set out from the beginning with a plan to integrate with other students, and to make friends. Student clubs and societies usually try to recruit new members at the beginning of the academic year in events named something like **'freshers' week'**. The UKCOSA report found that: 'Students who had participated in any type of activity on campus (for example joining clubs or societies, doing sport, drama, music, or volunteering) were more likely to have UK friends than those who had not'.
- *Mentoring.* This is also known as buddying, and many universities run schemes for students to link with other students who already know about life and studying here (either international or home students) so this can be

a way to break into this new culture. Often this sort of scheme runs for a period of a few weeks when new students first arrive and need to settle in. Hopefully, if your university runs this sort of scheme and you decide to join it, a mentor will contact you even before you leave home to travel. At the beginning they may simply show you around the university and nearby area so that you can find out quickly where the important facilities are, they could offer to describe their own experiences, perhaps to go to some social events together or to talk about some of the customs you may feel are strange.

- *Counselling.* This is a service supplied by specialist staff, usually in a department known as 'Student Services' or something similar. Counselling services do not tell you what to do when you have a problem, but they will listen to your difficulties and encourage you to make your own decisions. The Student Services will also have specialist professional services such as health centres, so find out about what they have to offer early on in your stay.

Task 1.10   Portfolio task

At the beginning of the chapter you looked at a list of possible life changes connected with moving to live and study in a new setting, and you now need to make an action plan about how you will deal with these changes. Look again at those points (and any others you added), and for each one write at least one sentence beginning with 'I will . . .' to outline the actions you can take to prepare yourself for this change. Use some of the ideas covered in this chapter, but also your own ideas and suggestions which came out of the discussions you have had. Put this action plan into Part A of your portfolio.

	I will . . .
Leaving friends and family:	
Eating different food:	
Living in a strange town:	
Making new friends:	
Using a foreign language:	
Finding a place to live:	
Finding a job:	
Dealing with officials:	
Living in a different climate:	
Being alone:	
Any further anxieties you added:	

Reference

UKCOSA (2004) *Broadening Our Horizons*. London: UKCOSA.

2

What sort of changes will I need to make?

Theme: culture

Aims of this chapter

By the end of this chapter you will have:

- Examined the idea of cultures of learning.
- Found out about the culture of learning in English speaking universities.
- Learnt about a theory concerning different learning styles.
- Seen what changes other international students have made in their learning style.
- Examined your own preferred learning styles.
- Looked at an explanation of what an undergraduate degree should involve.

Introductory exercise: styles of learning

Before looking at the styles of learning you will find in English speaking universities it is a good idea to think about your own preferred style of learning: what do you like doing as a student?

Task 2.1   Examining your own preferences

First complete the following questionnaire about the way you usually like to study. Put this in Part B of your portfolio.

	Strongly agree	Agree	Disagree	Strongly disagree
I think teachers should explain things clearly to me, so I can learn what they know.				
I like discussing my ideas with other people and hearing their ideas.				
I think that exams are the best way to measure learning, so all courses should finish with an exam.				
I usually think about tasks and activities carefully before I start them.				
I like to learn things by doing them, so I don't usually bother following instructions.				
I think that it is good to memorize important information.				
I think that there is usually a right answer to most questions.				
I prefer to work alone; other people distract me when I am thinking.				
I like to do assignments quickly; I get my best ideas when I am under pressure.				
I think that class discussions are a waste of time, I want to hear what the teacher thinks, not other students.				
I like to have a textbook for each course, and to learn everything in the book.				
I think students should ask questions after class if they want to find out about things.				
I think students should ask questions in class if they want to find out about things.				

Task 2.2   Discussion in pairs

Compare your responses with another student or a friend. As you discuss try to explain your choices:

- Are they a result of previous experiences you have had?
- Are they a result of your own personal preferences?
- Do you use different methods in different situations?

Learning styles

The way a student studies is probably a result of several things, and in this chapter you will find out about three of the most important reasons.

- *Previous experiences*: this means the ways you have learnt to study, possibly since you were very young, and some of these ways have perhaps become habits. There are things you were praised for doing, and other things you were told you must not do. These may lead you to expect certain things, for example do you think students should listen silently in classes, and do you always expect to take examinations at the end of every course?
- *The requirements of the situation you are in*: even if you stay within one country there will still be different situations where you will use the particular methods needed in each situation. For example, can you remember any changes in learning methods you had to make when you moved from lower school to high school?
- *Your own personal preferences*: even with students from the same background there are always individual styles. For example if you buy a new piece of equipment do you first read the instructions or do you first try to work out how to use it yourself?

Previous experiences

Online readings: theories of culture

On the website www.openup.co.uk/internationalstudents connected to this course there are three readings which refer to theories of culture:

1   Hodgetts, A. and Luthans, F. (1997) *International Management*, 3rd edn. London: McGraw-Hill.

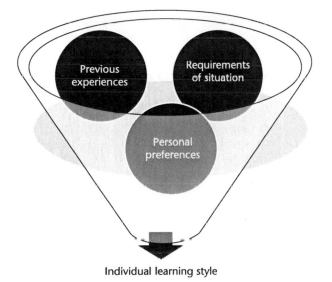

Individual learning style

Figure 2.1 Learning styles

2   Payne, N. (2007) *Intercultural Training and the Iceberg Model.* Online. South Petherton: Kwintessential. © Neil Payne, Kwintessential Ltd, 2007.
3   Crace, J. (2003) Crossing Culture. *Education Guardian.* Online. Tuesday, 14 October 2003.

Read through these three source texts, but read them quite quickly just to get a general understanding. You will find out more about techniques for reading for general information like this in Chapter 6. Then look at the text below.

The cultural iceberg

A common model used to illustrate the links of behaviour to culture uses the image of an iceberg (see Figure 2.2).

The upper part of the iceberg, above water, represents the behaviours you can observe, while the larger invisible part, under the water, includes things like beliefs, values, attitudes and your own idea of yourself; these are things which cannot be directly observed. Difficulties sometimes happen when we interpret the behaviours of people from other cultures using our own values and beliefs, and these can be different from theirs. Put simply, when we see people behaving in a certain way they may mean one thing but we can understand something very different. Universities are an example of organizational cultures where there are certain expected ways to behave, and

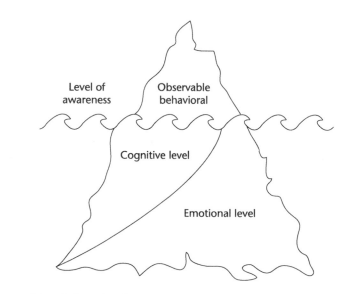

Level of awareness   Observable behavioral

Cognitive level

Emotional level

Figure 2.2   Cultural iceberg

interpretations of what certain behaviours mean. For example, teachers from a culture where people normally look directly at each other when they are talking (looking into each others' eyes) may think that a student who looks away from them is hiding something: the student – from another culture – may just be showing respect for the teacher.

Universities are cultures of learning, so universities in different settings may share some observable features (think of libraries, lecture theatres, the distinction between students and lecturers) but they may have very different hidden parts of the iceberg, for example very different ideas of what knowledge is and how learning should happen. That is what this book sets out to explore.

Learning tip   If you are going to study in another country you may need to learn another language, but more than that you will need to learn what you are expected to do during your studies (we will look at this in more detail in Part Two of this book) and how your work is going to be assessed (we will look at this in more detail in Part Three). Try to enjoy finding out about these differences, and be happy with the idea that things can be different without being either better or worse than the things you are used to.

Task 2.3 Discussion in pairs

Explain to another student what your own background in education is, covering these topics:

* How many hours each week did you spend in classes and lectures; what was a typical daily timetable?
* Were classes mixed, or were boys and girls educated separately; how big were the classes; what clothes did the students wear?
* What was the relationship between teachers and students: friendly, formal, strict?
* Did you often use group work in classes or for assessments?
* What forms of assessment were used: examinations, essays or anything else?
* Were you a good student?

The requirements of the situation

Here are the comments of some international students when they were asked about the changes they found in methods of studying when they came to a university in the UK. They talked about four things: the use of time; the relationship with tutors; the importance of group work and discussion; and the many different types of assessment they found in the UK.

Use of time

Student from China:

There's a really big difference, my feeling is in the UK the system encourages student to do research by themselves after the lectures, that's what you do most of the time. When you are doing an assignment you cannot just use the lecture notes, you must do research by yourself, so you can compare different people's opinion, and have your own opinion.

Student from France:

I use most of my time reading, I only have 12 hours in lectures and seminars each week, but I am in the final year and doing my **dissertation** now, so I spend most of my time just studying in the library.

Student from Czech Republic:

Here you only have a few hours in class, but you are expected to study 30 hours per week on your own.

Reliance on group work

Student from France:

> We use lots of **group work** here, much more than in France, for seminars and assessments like presentations. It's important to use discussions in seminars to know what the different opinions are. You have to say something, to contribute to the discussion. For a presentation first we meet in a group, decide what the topic was and how to go about it. We have to arrange these meetings outside of classes. There are also **student led seminars**, where the students organize activities for the group, and the tutor sits and watches your participation.

Student from Switzerland:

> Discussion is absolutely necessary, to confront the different ideas, you need to take them all together to have a point of view, and the feedback from different cultures is important and useful because there are not only English people here.

Assessments

Student from China:

> In the UK you learn to solve problems, you don't just remember a lot of things, the theory is important but you have to use the theories to solve problems. That's what the assessments are.

Student from Switzerland:

> I was only used to having examinations, no assignments to do out of class, so it's totally different. Here there are so many different types of assessments: presentations, reports, dissertations, designing web-pages, just so many. There are some examinations, but these are not the only method they use here.

Student from China:

> In my experience in the past at home the main way to test the outcome was with exams at the end of the two terms, so students could work hard just before the exams, but here the weight of the examinations is quite low, you have to keep working throughout the year.

Accessibility of tutors

Student from France:

> The relationship with tutors is very different here, in France the relationship is much more formal. Here students can address tutors by their

first name: 'John' or 'Wendy' and so on. Also tutors are much more available, you can drop by to their office, or send an email with a question you have.

Student from Switzerland:

The relationship with teachers is completely different, you are always in contact, can email, go to see them in the office, this is not possible at home, you have to find everything yourself without any help.

Learning tip   If you want to contact a tutor it is much better to send an email to ask for an appointment. Despite what these students said you should not just drop into their office, or stop them to ask questions at the end of lectures and seminars. Remember, though, to make these emails short and correctly written; they are not text messages to friends, approach them as a professional communication.

Task 2.4   The use of discussions

There is an adage that if two people give each other a pound they still only have only one pound each, but if they give each other an idea they each will have two ideas. For each of the following points – concerning *reasons* for seminar discussions, *requirements* of seminars, and *advice* about seminars – indicate if you agree or disagree with the views given.

These are some of the *reasons* for using seminar discussions as a method of learning:	
Most knowledge, particularly learning which involves language in any way at all, comes from discussing with other people.	AGREE/DISAGREE
By discussing you can see other points of view.	AGREE/DISAGREE
Discussion helps you to clarify your own ideas (and change your ideas).	AGREE/DISAGREE
Seminar participation can sometimes be assessed. If you do not join in the discussions you will lose marks.	AGREE/DISAGREE
Seminar participation can develop the skills of working with others.	AGREE/DISAGREE

These are some of the *requirements* of seminar discussions as a method of learning:	
Usually you need to prepare for seminars, for example to read course notes/readings.	AGREE/DISAGREE
Usually you need to prepare questions which you want to explore.	AGREE/DISAGREE
You must participate in the discussions to share the work of creating the knowledge of the group.	AGREE/DISAGREE
If you listen without talking you are taking without giving.	AGREE/DISAGREE
You must listen as well as speak, and you must invite the opinions of others.	AGREE/DISAGREE
Here is some *advice* about seminar discussions:	
All people can be nervous of giving their opinions, but the more you participate the easier it will become for you.	AGREE/DISAGREE
Make sure you say something, even if it is things like: *Sorry, can you explain that again? Can you give an example of that? Yes, I agree with you.*	AGREE/DISAGREE
Clearly say if you agree or disagree with others in the group, but be polite.	AGREE/DISAGREE
Build up you participation by pushing yourself to say more in every seminar.	AGREE/DISAGREE

Learning activities in English speaking universities

First, we will look broadly at the structure of most undergraduate courses and at three types of activities which most students in English universities use on a daily basis: **lectures**, seminars, and **virtual learning environments (VLEs)**.

Structure of undergraduate courses

Most university undergraduate degree courses last for three years, although some students may need to do a foundation year before that, and some international students may transfer from universities at home and so join a degree in its second or third year, for example in 'top-up' degrees. Different universities organize the academic year differently, for example in some universities the year may be divided into two semesters and students will study perhaps four modules in each semester, while in other universities they may study six modules throughout the complete academic year. A module covers a topic area, so for example a first year student of marketing may have different modules such as:

- Foundations of marketing
- Introduction to marketing communications
- Accounting information systems
- Tomorrow's consumers
- The business environment
- Economics of the real world

> **Learning tip** Your main activity as a student will always be to read, and if you do not do the necessary reading then you will probably not be able to follow the lectures. You must get into the habit of reading extensively in English, and reading skills will be covered in Chapters 6 and 9 of this book. Begin now to set yourself a daily target, begin to read for one hour everyday, and then increase the target week by week.

Typically a student will have one lecture and one seminar for each module each week, but neither lectures nor seminars are like school lessons where the teacher gives facts for students to learn. Both the lectures and the seminars are based on the expectation that you are familiar with the ideas which have come out of your reading. So what are the differences between lectures and seminars?

Lectures

In the lectures the lecturer will often supply a commentary of the many theories in that module's subject area, to show how they are connected, for example how some key thinkers developed the ideas of earlier thinkers, or how one school of thought differs from another. In lectures there may be over 100 students who usually listen, probably for one hour, and often the lecturer uses tools such as PowerPoint presentations or electric whiteboards.

Seminars

Seminars involve students in the discussion, they are smaller (usually 15–20 students), and often seminars follow the lecture. They may last for one or two hours. Seminars often have some kind of task, for example in business schools you may discuss case studies of companies, and in media courses you may discuss a film you have all seen. Seminars demand student participation, the object is to hear diverse views. They are also opportunities to ask for clarifications from questions you may have as a result of your reading and the lecture, or about assessment requirements.

VLEs

Many modules now are supported by virtual learning environments, which are on a university's intranet. Tutors use these to communicate with students, to post activities and case studies for you to read, or to link you to course readings. These VLEs can also have discussion boards where students can exchange ideas, for example when they are doing group work. Many lecturers will post their PowerPoint slides from lectures on the VLE, so if you find that your lecturers do this you do not need to copy these slides during the lecture and instead can concentrate on listening to what the lecturer is saying.

> **Learning tip** When you are at university do not think about 'answering' questions, it is always better to think about 'discussing' questions. Be prepared to find that there is almost never a single agreed answer to any question, but a range of different 'schools of thought' which you will need to evaluate. This idea of evaluation will be developed throughout this book.

Task 2.5   Portfolio task

Use the chart below to make notes to compare your own educational background (recalling ideas you thought of in Task 2.3) with ideas from the students' descriptions of English universities you read above and the description of typical learning activities in English speaking universities. Then add a plan about how you will be able to deal with any changes.
Copy the completed chart into Part B of your portfolio.

	Previous experience	UK universities
Use of time / daily timetable		
Plan for change	I will . . .	
Relationship with tutors		
Plan for change	I will . . .	
Use of group work		
Plan for change	I will . . .	
Methods of assessment		
Plan for change	I will . . .	

Personal preferences

There are many explanations of different learning styles, for example one popular model divides people into those who:

- Prefer to see things, for example watching demonstrations or having written explanations (visual style).
- Prefer to hear and discuss instructions (auditory style).
- Like to try things out by doing them (kinaesthetic style).

Think about your own style: do you think you fit into one of these groups?

Task 2.6   Pair work

In pairs, do the following exercise which uses a learning style questionnaire. Remember, however, that the **VAK (visual, auditory and kinaesthetic) model** is just one of many models, and so there are many different classifications of learning styles. This type of activity is really just a way for you to notice that there are different ways of thinking and solving problems. It is not really a scientific analysis, so treat it as fun – but as a fun activity from which you can learn something.

Learning styles questionnaire

Ask another student which of the following choices they normally make in the following situations, and for each question discuss any differences between your answers.

1   **You have just bought a new MP3 player (which is also a USB storage device and FM radio). Do you:**

(a) Read the instructions which came with the device?

(b) Ask a friend to tell you how it works?

(c) Start to use it at once, to try to work it out for yourself?

2   **You are on a day trip to Cambridge and you want to find one specific college. Do you:**

(a) Buy a map of the city so you can find your way around?

(b) Stop someone on the street and ask for directions?

(c) Just walk around the streets trying to find the place, perhaps looking for street signs?

3   **You want to learn how to cook a dish which you enjoyed eating in a restaurant. Do you:**

(a) Use Google to find a recipe for the dish on the Internet?

(b) Ask a friend who is a good cook how to cook it?

(c) Remember the dish and try to recreate it, to experiment until you find an okay way of doing it?

4   **Your friend has asked you how to use PowerPoint. Do you:**

(a) Find a guide of step-by-step instructions your friend can read?

(b) Speak to them, to tell them what are the important things to remember?

(c) Sit with them at a PC and demonstrate?

5   **Imagine you have upset a close friend by not keeping a promise you made. Your friend tells you that s/he is upset. Do you say:**

(a) I see what you mean.

(b) I hear what you say.

(c) I know how you feel.

6 **Your boss wants you to do a new task, something you have never done before. Do you say:**

(a) Show me how you want me to do it.

(b) Tell me how you want me to do it.

(c) Let me have a try and I'll ask if I need help.

7 **Your young nephew is learning how to play a new computer game. Do you say:**

(a) Watch me, I'll show you how it's done.

(b) Listen to me, I'll explain it to you.

(c) Go on, you try, let me watch.

8 **Your new MP3 player is not working correctly. Do you:**

(a) Write a letter of complaint to the shop/manufacturer?

(b) Telephone the shop/manufacturer to tell them what the problem is?

(c) Go to the shop to complain and ask for a replacement?

9 **You have been asked to organize a social event for a group of students so they can get to know each other better. Do you plan:**

(a) A trip to a museum or gallery?

(b) A night out in a pub so you can chat?

(c) A session of paintballing?

10 **It's the birthday of one of your friends. Do you decide to buy:**

(a) A new novel by an author you know she likes?

(b) A CD of her favourite band?

(c) Some software you know she needs?

11 **You need to buy a smart outfit to go to a job interview. Do you:**

(a) Look at the clothes in the shop and imagine whether they will look good on you?

(b) Ask the sales assistant whether she thinks they suit you?

(c) Try them on?

12 **You are going to buy a new car and need to choose between four. Do you:**

(a) Read about the advantages and disadvantages of the possible cars in auto magazines?

(b) Ask your friends which car they think is best?

(c) Ask the garage if you can have a test drive?

Total for (a)	Mostly (a) = a preference for a visual learning style.
Total for (b)	Mostly (b) = a preference for an auditory learning style.
Total for (c)	Mostly (c) = a preference for a kinaesthetic/physical/ tactile learning style.

Learning tip   The way we each like to learn is, in part, a result of our individual character and, in part, a result of previous experiences we have had as students.

- Remember, though, that not all people from one culture do things in exactly the same way.
- Remember that all people can use a variety of learning styles.
- Remember that people can and do change how they learn as a result of new experiences and new opportunities.

What a UK university degree involves

The Quality Assurance Agency (QAA) is an organization which checks academic standards and quality in universities in the UK, and it gives the following description of what an undergraduate honours degree should represent. We will refer to this description several times in this book to explain why we do the things we do. Read it several times, consulting a dictionary to check any words that you are unsure of:

> An Honours graduate will have developed an understanding of a complex body of knowledge, some of it at the current boundaries of an academic discipline. Through this, the graduate will have developed analytical techniques and problem-solving skills that can be applied in many types of employment. The graduate will be able to evaluate evidence, arguments and assumptions, to reach sound judgements, and to communicate effectively. . . . An Honours graduate should have the qualities needed for employment in situations requiring the exercise of personal responsibility, and decision-making in complex and unpredictable circumstances.
>
> (QAA 2001)

Task 2.7   Small group discussion

Many of these ideas will be explored more deeply later in this book, but now discuss in small groups what you understand by these phrases. Then number them from 1 to 5, where 1 is what you consider to be the most important and 5 the least important:

- The current boundaries of an academic discipline. ☐
- Analytical techniques and problem solving skills. ☐
- Evaluate evidence, arguments and assumptions. ☐
- To communicate effectively. ☐
- Decision making in complex and unpredictable circumstances. ☐

Task 2.8 Portfolio task

When people discuss moving between different cultures they often use the concept of 'culture shock' and this will be examined in the next chapter. You should not forget, however, that most of the experience of living and studying in a different country is positive, exciting, and an opportunity to grow and develop. Write a short essay about what your plans and hopes are for your period of studying abroad: what do you want to study; how long will you stay; what are your personal goals during this time? Write around 300 words.

Reference

QAA (Quality Assurance Agency) (2001) *The Framework for Higher Education Qualifications in England, Wales and Northern Ireland: January 2001*. London: QAA. Available at: http://www.qaa.ac.uk/academicinfrastructure/FHEQ/EWNI/default.asp

3

What sort of things will I have to do?

Theme: adaptation

Aims of this chapter

By the end of this chapter you will have:

- Seen how different students use their time for different activities.
- Explored the idea of having a balanced life.
- Seen why you should explore the society and culture you will be living in.
- Found out more about students' unions.
- Looked at reasons for volunteering and types of volunteering.
- Looked at self-management skills for independent living.
- Explored the factors necessary for healthy living.
- Discussed advice concerning culture shock.
- Looked at how to carry out ethnographic research.

Introductory exercise: how do you use your time?

Most of this book is about studying, but the focus of this chapter is about getting a good balance between studying and other aspects of your life. You will not just be studying in the country you are going to, you will also be living there, so you need to have plans for all aspects of your life. Before you look at the life-styles of some students at one of the universities in the UK it is a good idea to examine how you use your time at the moment. The pie chart below (Figure 3.1) was made by one student to show how, on average, she divides up her time. The categories she used were: 'sleep', 'study', 'social', 'cooking etc.', and 'other'.

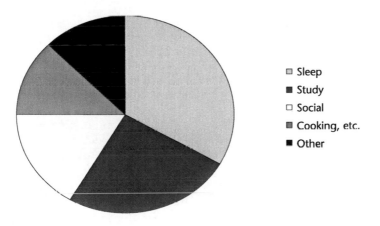

- ▢ Sleep
- ▪ Study
- ▢ Social
- ▨ Cooking, etc.
- ▪ Other

Figure 3.1   Use of time

Task 3.1   Charting your own use of time

Now make a similar pie chart yourself by first listing the different things you did each day for the last week. You may want to use the same categories as the student in Figure 3.1 or you can create different categories, for example if you spend a lot of time each day travelling, or if you do a lot of sport, these may be categories which are significant for you.

Task 3.2   Small group discussion

Now show each other your pie charts and make constructive comments. For example if one student spends more time playing computer games than studying, what suggestions can you give? If another student spends lots of time studying and no time relaxing, what advice can you give?

Living tip   At some universities it is possible for students to spend all of their time on the campus as you can find everything you need close at hand: your accommodation, a supermarket, shops, restaurants, sports facilities and so on. However, if you always remain on campus you will miss the opportunity of finding out about the culture and society of the place you have come to live in – so make sure you can plan ways to go out and explore.

A day in the life . . .

In this chapter you will look at a typical day in the life of four students who live in a house near a university about 50 miles north of London. Their house is typical of the kind that students share in many parts of the UK: it is a terraced house, which was built around 100 years ago, and each student has their own bedroom, but they share the kitchen, living room and bathroom. You might want to compare this with the accommodation of the students you saw in Chapter 1 who were living on campus, and think which style would be best for you. These four students have come from different countries and study different courses, so they did not know each other before they started to share this house. Sometimes, though, the four of them arrange to spend an afternoon at home when they first clean the house together, then in the evening they take turns to cook a meal. While they eat they tell each other about what they are doing at that time. It is now Sunday evening, and they are in the kitchen talking about what they have to do on Monday.

Student A comes from the north of England and she is doing the second year of a degree in a business school

I'm going to go into the university as early as I can tomorrow, and then I'll spend the morning studying in the IT centre. Two of my modules are using **online groups**, so I've got to check the **discussion boards** to find out what the other students are doing and planning. In one of my modules we are researching about customer satisfaction with products connected to IT – things like mobile phones, SatNavs, and MP3s. I've got to look at some online journals to find articles on that sort of topic; and one of the other group members is looking at manufacturers' websites to find what they claim about their products. The third guy is beginning to design a questionnaire we can use with consumers to see if they feel products they have bought are as good as they expected. We have to record what we are doing every week on the module online discussion board so the tutor can keep track of how we are working, and then we have to write a report about the whole project at the end of the semester. For the other module we each have to write a **blog**; the module is about advertising and we each have to evaluate one TV ad every week and post our comments about it on the blog, which means I have to watch TV to find an ad which is interesting. You also have to read everybody else's blog so we can give each other feedback in the seminar discussion. That really takes a lot of time, but you have to do it because we get marked on our participation in seminars.

   At lunchtime tomorrow I'm going to spend an hour in the uni gym, I try to do that three times a week and I really feel much better after working out, I can forget about my course while doing press-ups. In the afternoon I'm going for an interview for a part-time job in a call centre, I hope I can get it, not just because I need the money but also because I want to spend next year doing a work-placement before I do the last year of my degree, and I know this company has some opportunities for placement students. I really must go to the hairdressers before the interview if I have time. Tonight I've got to check and print out my CV to take with me. After that, tomorrow night, I'm going to the Students' Union bar to meet some of my friends, and if I do get the job we can celebrate together.

Task 3.3   Discussion in pairs

Discuss this student's day with another student: is there anything surprising in it?

In other chapters we examine more deeply these study points connected to Student A's day:

- Doing primary research (Chapter 8).
- Using and evaluating online sources (Chapter 9).
- Having online assessments (Chapter 4).
- Participating in seminars (Chapter 2).
- Doing part time work and work placements (Chapter 1).
- Preparing CVs (Chapter 11).

Students' unions

Student A talks about meeting her friends in the students' union. You will find that a lot of social life in universities revolves around the students' union, which you become a member of when you enter a university. There are many facets of these organizations: they run sports clubs and social events, and they have restaurants, cafes and bars in just about every university. The students' unions are run by and for students, and they are concerned with improving all parts of students' lives.

Living tip   Some international students might not want to go into bars, pubs and clubs because they do not drink alcohol – but don't worry, you will find that all these places also have soft drinks and hot drinks like tea and coffee. One of the best ways to integrate with classmates is to 'go for a coffee' after the lecture in the Union, particularly at the beginning of a course when all students (not just international students) are looking for friends.

Task 3.4   Online reading

The link below is for the National Union of Students in England. First explore the site at http://www.nus.org.uk/en/ and find the help and advice it has to offer about student life.

Then from this site you can link to the students' union of any particular university or college. If you already know the university you are going to attend then follow the link to find information about the students' union there. If you are not certain where you will go, follow two or three of the links to get an idea of the type of support and events these unions run.

Living tip   Many universities encourage new students to contact existing students by email before they arrive. If you can find a contact then don't just ask about courses and studying, also find out what social and cultural opportunities there are.

Student B: she is an exchange student from Switzerland and is studying in a school of education

Monday is always my really busy day for lectures and seminars; I have half of my week's sessions all on one day. Tomorrow morning should be interesting because last week we all went to visit different primary schools, so tomorrow each student has to give a summary of one aspect of the school we visited so we can see how different theories of education are put into practice. It's not a formal presentation assessment, but later in the semester we each will have to make a poster to summarize our visits and that will be an assessment. So tomorrow the feedback we get from the others will help us to decide which things are most important and interesting. Later tonight, before I go to bed, I am going to choose the photos I will show the others – I am going to concentrate on the methods they used to teach reading, I think it's very different from what I am used to in primary schools at home. In the afternoon I will have two lectures, and I always get really tired trying to concentrate and make notes because English is a foreign language for me, but the lecturers put their notes on the VLE so I can check them later to see if I missed anything important. I'm still going to be busy in the evening, I've started to do some voluntary work with old people, and tomorrow I'm going to visit one old man I read to every week. I quite like doing that, he is very friendly and it is a good way to find out more about the culture here, in fact sometimes it's difficult for me to get away because he can talk for hours and hours about when he was young. If I'm not too late getting home, and if I'm not too tired after doing all that, I will do some course reading: I try to do at least two hours everyday.

Task 3.5   Discussion in pairs

Discuss this day with another student: what do you think about the voluntary work she does; would you want to do something similar?

In other chapters we examine more deeply these study points connected to Student B's day:

- Understanding the differences of lectures and seminars (Chapter 2).
- Applying theories in practice (Chapter 9).
- Receiving and acting on feedback (Chapter 4).
- Completing different types of assessment (Chapter 4).
- Making comparisons with previous experience (Introduction).
- Taking notes in lectures (Chapter 7).
- Checking course VLE (Chapter 2).
- Reading extensively (Chapter 5).

Volunteering

You saw in the previous chapter that volunteering is a good way to develop skills and so can be useful for your future career, but there are many other good reasons for volunteering:

- You can meet different people (like the old man described by Student B) and so you can integrate with people.
- You can make friends with other volunteers.
- It is enjoyable; you feel that you are doing something worthwhile.
- It helps you to develop confidence by having responsibilities and making decisions.
- It can give you ideas about how you want to develop later on in your life.

Living tip   Most universities will have a volunteer bureau, and they will have introductory sessions during your induction period. You will find that they have a lot of different types of opportunities: working with children or the elderly; doing environmental projects; helping in charity shops. See this as a way to make friends and to find out more about the culture of the country you are living in.

Task 3.6   Online reading

CSV is one of the largest volunteering agencies in the UK. First read through some of the links at http://www.csv.org.uk/ to get a general idea about the things this organization does. Then use the 'Quick links' to read about one type of volunteering, for example 'Health and Social Care' or 'Environment', and read the information you find.

Task 3.7   Pair work

Explain to another student what you think about this type of volunteering: do you think you would like to do it; do you think it would be a good way to integrate into society; do you think it would be interesting?

Student C comes from Scotland and he is his final year in geography and environmental management

The first thing I do every morning is to go for a five mile run, it helps me to think about what I am going to do during the day, and also if I miss the run I find it harder to get to sleep at night. One thing I must do tomorrow is to try to meet with my tutor; I'm trying to sort out a suitable topic for my dissertation, because I've got to start working on that before the end of the month. It's going to take me four months to plan it, to do the research, and then to write it up. We went on a **field trip** last year to look at a water management scheme in Spain, and I want to do some more research on the same topic and use that for the dissertation, but I need my tutor to give me some suggestions about suitable research methods. I've really got to start doing the **literature review**, so I need to start to do a lot of reading about water management in different books and articles. Also tomorrow I am going to have a **time constrained test** in one of my geography modules about satellite imaging. They will give us the information at 11 o'clock and then we have four hours to think about it and collect information, so at 3 o'clock we go to the seminar room and have one hour to write the answers. I haven't done this type of test before so I hope I can work out what to do, but it's really an exciting module as the topic is so up to date. In fact I think I would like to get a job related to satellite imaging when I graduate, and I want to talk to my tutor and the Careers Service about that. In the evening I've got to go to the supermarket to do some shopping because I've invited my girlfriend and two of her flatmates to come for dinner; they've invited me to dinner a few times recently so I need to return the favour.

Task 3.8   Discussion in pairs

Discuss Student C's day with another student: do you already have plans about the type of work you would like to do after graduating? If you do, have you started to do things which will help you get that sort of work?

In other chapters we examine more deeply these study points connected to Student C's day:

- Completing dissertations (Chapter 4).
- Contacting tutors (Chapter 2).
- Writing a literature review (Chapter 4).
- Using a range of types of articles (Chapter 9).
- Studying up to date ideas, the latest technology (Chapter 2).
- Linking your studies to employment (Chapter 2).
- Consulting careers services (Chapter 1).

Self-management

Student C is going to cook a meal for some friends, and you have seen that all the students in this house regularly cook for each other. This is one example of the essential life skills that all people need to live independently, but you may not have developed these skills if your parents have always looked after you, or if you have lived in a school where everything is organized for you.

Task 3.9   Assessing your life skills

How confident are you about your own life skills? Imagine you are living in this house with these students. Number the tasks below from one to ten, where 1 = 'I feel most confident' and 10 = 'I feel least confident'. Put this in Part B of your portfolio:

- Planning a meal / shopping / cooking.
- Managing your finances / making a weekly budget / paying bills.
- Washing clothes.
- Travelling independently / going abroad / travelling around the country you will study in.
- Living harmoniously with a group of other people.
- Sharing jobs in the house / cleaning the kitchen, bathroom and toilet (students not having servants).
- Getting medical help / making an appointment with a dentist.
- Making a complaint, for example in a shop.
- Keeping your own room clean.
- Organizing your day/week.

Task 3.10 Making an action plan

Now show your self-assessment to another student. Starting with the skill you feel the least confident about, discuss how you can improve that skill; for example if you cannot cook now how can you learn some recipes?

Living tip It is a good idea to ask someone who knows you well (for example your parents) what they think about your independent living skills; they may know you better than you know yourself.

Student D comes from China and arrived recently to complete a final year top-up in business computing after studying a diploma in Beijing

I'm going to stay in my room in the morning to read, I have to spend so long reading because English is not my first language, so I think I should spend three or four hours everyday to keep up with my courses. Often I do a lot of reading at the weekend but next weekend I am going to visit one of my old friends from high school who is now studying in Wales, so this week I have to do a lot of reading. In the afternoon I have a lecture and then a two-hour seminar; we are doing a group task about project management and looking for reasons why large IT projects often fail. That is really useful for me because the other students in the group all speak English much better than me, but they think I am more expert in a lot of computing things so they want to learn from me. They ask a lot of technical questions and I really enjoy trying to explain these difficult things in English. I am lucky because we all get on very well. I've just organized a team of these class-mates to take part in a 6 a-side football league, so tomorrow night we are going to a local sports centre for our first game. I hope this will be fun even if we never win, and I think this is something which will look good on my CV because setting up the team and contacting the league organizers really made me think about how to manage people and how to communicate in a lot of different ways. When I come back home after the game I will try to do some more reading, I will need to go through the topics for Tuesday's lectures because there is always new vocabulary for every topic.

Task 3.11 Discussion in pairs

Discuss this day with another student: is there anything Student D does which you think you will try to copy?

At different parts of this book we examine the following points connected to Student D's day:

- Learning autonomously (Chapter 6).
- Doing group work (Chapter 8).
- Developing your CV (Chapter 11).
- Developing communication skills (Chapter 4).
- Working with people skills (Chapter 4).
- Developing subject specific vocabulary (Chapter 7).

Doing sport and living healthily

Several of these students mention doing sport or some kind of physical activity and they each talk about different reasons for this:

- Student A says: 'I really feel much better after working out, I can forget about my course while doing press-ups'.
- Student C says: 'I . . . go for a five mile run, it helps me to think about what I am going to do during the day, and also if I miss the run I find it harder to get to sleep at night'.
- Student D says: 'we are going to a local sports centre for our first game. I hope this will be fun even if we never win'.

> **Living tip** If you can, depending on your health and physical condition, you should also try to have some form of regular exercise. This can be something organized like a team sport, or it can just be about taking healthy choices such as walking to the shops instead of taking the bus. It can also be a social opportunity, for example going to a swimming pool with friends. Do not forget to check out sports clubs at the students' union.

Task 3.12 Online reading and reflection

Use an Internet search engine and the key words: 'healthy body healthy mind', look through several of the sites you find, then look back to the pie chart you made at the beginning of this chapter and decide if you should change any of your habits.

> **Living tip** If you smoke, stop.

Culture shock

Eating well, doing sport, sleeping properly, feeling that you have friends – these are all part of a well balanced life (also remember the hierarchy of needs you looked at in Chapter 1). When you move to a new situation it is possible that you will initially have problems finding this balance, and this increases the chances of you sometimes feeling unhappy, or experiencing what some people call **culture shock**. In Chapter 1 you found out a little about an organization, UKCISA, which is concerned with the well being of international students, and saw that it offers advice to international students on a lot of topics. Here is the URL where you can find advice concerning culture shock: http://www.ukcosa.org.uk/files/pdf/info_sheets/culture_shock.pdf

Task 3.13   Group discussion

Go through the UKCISA advice about culture shock; discuss what it is, and how you will deal with this kind of situation.

Living tip   Notice that the UKCISA advice sheet explains that different people have different experiences, so you should not expect that you will certainly have a difficult time. You may find that everything is fine from the beginning. However, if you do sometimes feel a bit down the advice they give is certainly worth following.

Looking forward: ethnography

The approach to learning about education in UK universities which this book takes is based on looking at a university as being an example of a community with its own culture, and also seeing that the university is located in a society which also has its own culture. You found out in Chapter 2 that we can observe behaviours but we cannot observe beliefs, values and attitudes. You saw that difficulties sometimes happen when we interpret other people's behaviours using our own values and beliefs which can be different from theirs. The fact that things like assumptions and beliefs are taken for granted by the members of a culture means that they simply do not notice them, in the same way that we do not notice the oxygen we breathe. Outsiders, however, can notice if there are differences between their own original culture and the new culture they are observing. If you set out to study a new culture, to observe it, reflect on it, and try to work out the rules which the participants follow, then you are following an approach known as **ethnography**. You will find out more at methods of researching in Chapter 8. The approach taken in this book, therefore, is an ethnographic approach, and we will look at this concept in a little more detail now.

What is ethnography?

This approach to research began in social anthropology, when people were trying to understand societies very different to their own. More recently ethnography has developed as a method of research in many areas such as business organizations, health care, criminology and education. Ethnographers try to understand how people in a culture (such as the culture inside a company or a university) identify themselves and their roles. The ethnographer is an outsider who takes part in the daily life of this situation, and so is engaged in long and close contact with the setting they are studying. Therefore it is a suitable approach for international students, because you may stay for several years, to understand the cultures they find in the country they are visiting.

This is a summary of the methods that ethnographers use:

- They observe people operating as groups.
- They observe them over a long period of time.
- They try to understand what these people they are observing think and believe.
- They write an explanation of what happens.

Living tip   Try to use ideas of ethnographic research while you are getting to know more about this new culture you are entering. If you take this positive approach then you will understand better the culture of the university, and as a result your own adaptation to this new, and we hope exciting, environment will be easier. Do not see the behaviours of the teachers and students around you as just being strange or different, instead recognize them as evidence for you to collect and consider in order to work out the framework of ideas and beliefs that underlie this culture.

Task 3.14 Group discussion

In small groups think of different groups of people you will be able to observe during your stay at university (you have already seen lots of these situations in this book). Think of both academic and social situations where you will be able to observe people talking to each other and getting things done, this could be simple things like paying for shopping, getting advice, or more complicated sessions such as groups of students in seminars or informally chatting over meals.

Task 3.15   Portfolio task

Imagine that you are going to do some ethnographic research involving one of the students we have seen in this chapter. You have read a description of a typical day of that student and now you want to interview her or him to find out more about why they do the things they do, and the groups they are in. You are trying to come to conclusions about the rules of social interaction they follow. Write several questions which you could ask this student, remember that the intention is to find out what this student thinks and believes, so the questions should be quite open (that is, not asking for yes/no answers), and they should encourage the student to talk about their feelings and ideas. Put these questions in Part B of your portfolio.

4

What sort of assessments will I have?

Theme: assessment

Aims of this chapter

By the end of this chapter you will have:

- Explored different principles of assessment.
- Seen the difference between declarative knowledge and functional knowledge.
- Explored the idea of **key skills (transferable skills)**.
- Explored different approaches to assessment.
- Become familiar with some of the most common types of assessment.

Introductory exercise: educational milestones

Most people's educational career is marked by certain important moments, for example when you leave one class or school and move on to the next stage; we can think of these as educational milestones. Often these moments involve some form of assessment, which can influence our whole lives depending on whether we pass or fail.

Task 4.1   Small group discussion

In small groups you should describe what have been the key milestones in your own education, and tell each other what the assessments connected to these consisted of, and how you felt at the time. If you are discussing with students from another culture then ask questions to clarify things which are different, and discuss the differences you find.

The principles of assessment

Matching intended learning outcomes (ILOs) with assessment tasks

The first principle of assessment is that students should know from the beginning of any course what they should be learning and how they are going to be assessed. So before you examine different types of assessments it is a good idea to be clear about what all assessments are trying to measure. In Chapter 2 you saw a description of what undergraduate honours degrees should represent, and saw that this includes learning complex and up to date knowledge, which you can use to analyse and solve problems so that you can apply what you have learned in work situations. In order to achieve these intentions all university courses therefore must have clear **intended learning outcomes (ILOs)** which explain what you should know and be able to do as a result of studying this particular course. The ILOs will be described in **module and course guides**, and then the assessments you do during your courses are designed to find out if you have achieved these outcomes.

Learning tip   The word 'assignment' refers to any specific task someone is told to do, and the word 'assessment' refers to any form of valuing or measuring success. So when a student is given any piece of work to do this is an assignment, and if it is going to be marked or graded it will also be an assessment. It is important that you understand that there are a large number of types of assessment, and that new methods of assessing students are being designed constantly.

Here is one example of Intended Learning Outcomes taken from a short module concerning Human Resource Management:

On successful completion of the module students will be able to:

Knowledge and understanding

- Identify different purposes and goals of different types of organizations.
- Identify different forms of organizations and structures of organizations.
- Identify different models of communication.

Subject-specific skills

- Evaluate how communication can be managed by organizations.
- Identify the prime channels of communication in an organization.
- Identify problems associated with communications in different organizations.
- Explore potential solutions to communication problems.

Key skills

- Identify and reflect upon individual learning experiences and develop awareness of learning strategies by keeping a learning portfolio.
- Interact effectively with other students on an extended project, give and receive information, listen actively and speak effectively, and communicate effectively in written reports.
- Manage time effectively.

---

learning tip At the beginning of every course or module you are studying you should look for this clear description of the intended learning outcomes. You will find these in course or module guides, and often the guides will be on the course VLE. It is essential that you understand what each course sets out to achieve so you can assess whether or not you are meeting these outcomes.

Task 4.2   Small group discussion

At the end of the Introduction to this book you will find the ILOs of this course. In small groups, go through the list one by one and discuss if these intended outcomes are what you want to get from using this book. If you have any further needs not covered in this book then discuss how you can get information and find opportunities to practise these extra needs. Make notes about these extra needs and put the notes in Part A of your portfolio.

Identifying declarative knowledge, functional knowledge and key skills

The next principle of assessment is that the types of knowledge you need to demonstrate should also be made clear. The outcomes of a course can include some key facts that you should remember and be able to explain (this is often called declarative knowledge) but the main outcomes are usually about knowing how to do things (this is often called functional knowledge). All of your assignments are therefore designed so you can demonstrate that you have achieved these intended outcomes, which will usually involve you actually using information (for example making recommendations to solve a problem) instead of just repeating information. In addition to the knowledge and skills directly related to the subject of your degree, the intended learning outcomes for many courses often include mention of students developing key skills (or transferable skills) which link what you are studying now to your future employability. These refer to the skills that people need in any employment regardless of their specific job or profession: it doesn't matter if you are going to be an engineer, a teacher, or a nurse you will still be expected to possess these skills.

Task 4.3   Pair work

The following table refers to different aspects of an assignment given to a group of students doing a **project** together. The project involves the groups first investigating the methods of internal communication which are used in a large manufacturing company, then they have to decide how the communications can be improved, and after that they have to write a report and give an oral presentation describing their recommendations. Match the key skill in column one with the aspects of the assignment in column 2; you may find that some aspects require more than one key skill.

Key skills	Aspects of assignment
Communication. This connects to the ability to make yourself understood and also to understand others.	Producing graphs to show the percentages of staff who are satisfied with their company's methods of communicating information.
Application of number. This connects to using maths, for example to solve problems.	Interviewing a range of staff about their opinions of the methods of communication inside their company.
Information technology. This connects to the everyday uses of computers.	Completing this group project successfully: doing the research; writing the report; giving a presentation.
Working with others. This connects both to the teams you work in, and also the customers or clients your organization works with.	Devising recommendations concerning possible improvements to communication channels.

Key skills	Aspects of assignment
Improving own learning and performance. This connects to the ideas of reflective learning and life long learning.	Using PowerPoint to give an oral presentation about the group's findings.
Problem solving. This connects to application of knowledge to specific situations.	Keeping an individual reflective portfolio and a group log (recording meetings; allocation of responsibilities) of the project.

Task 4.4   Portfolio task

Another key skill you need to develop is the ability to assess yourself, and then to use your **self-assessment** to produce your own plan of how you will further develop your skills. For each of the following particular skills write a short summary of how you assess your own ability now, and then identify what you can do to further develop that particular skill. Put this in Part B of your portfolio.

- Using PowerPoint.
- Giving an oral presentation.
- Interviewing people.
- Working in a team.
- Writing reports.
- Making recommendations.
- Producing graphs.
- Writing reflections.

Providing clear assignment instructions

Another principle of assessment concerns the clarity of the assignment instructions. A very common reason for failing assessments is a student not analysing the task properly and so not doing what is expected. In order to be clear, the instructions for any assignment may be quite detailed, and so you will need to take time to understand them. Here is a simplified example of assignment instructions taken from a module in marketing which you will use again in Chapter 9:

Assignment brief

The concepts of developing brands and of brand management are well established in commercial areas such as food retailing, fast food restaurants and clothing. Most such companies invest heavily in creating and defending a brand image to differentiate themselves from their competitors. However, more recently there has been a growing understanding that charities (not for profit organizations) need also to build and manage their brands in order to compete with other charities for public attention and donations. For this assignment you are going to analyse a charity's current use of branding, then to carry out some primary research to discover how effective its branding strategy is. You will then write a report for the senior managers of that charity to recommend improvements you believe it should make. You need to choose which charity you are going to analyse and then notify your tutor of your choice before you start the primary research.

In this assignment you should first explain why concepts such as brand identity and brand image are important, and report on recently published research to explain why these concepts are also important for charities. In addition you need to demonstrate application of your learning; you should choose one example of a charity and analyse the communications it uses, then conduct some primary research using either a quantitative survey or qualitative interviews. In your report you should comment critically on this charity's use of branding. You need also to make recommendations of how this charity can improve its public profile.

For this assignment you should use a report format: a title page; a contents page; an executive summary; theoretical background; the case study; your findings from primary research; your recommendations. You should write a maximum of 1500 words. You should follow the Harvard referencing system and include a list of references. Any examples of the charity communications should be included as an appendix and are not included in the word count.

Note: this is only a simple example; expect the assignments on your degree courses to be far more complex than this.

As well as clear instructions the assignment will have a clear marking scheme, telling you how the marks will be allocated for doing different things. This will be linked to your university assessment criteria which you will find out about in Chapter 10.

Task 4.5   Small group discussion

Decide if the following points taken from the assignment brief above are: *declarative knowledge* (being able to demonstrate knowledge of theory); *functional knowledge* (being able to use knowledge to do things); or *key skills* (abilities which you can apply in many situations).

- Explaining the concept of brand management.
- Analysing a charity's current use of branding.
- Writing a report.
- Recommending improvements.
- Analysing a charity's communications.

- Carrying out interviews.
- Including a list of references.

Application activities

Another principle of university assessments is that assignments will require you to find **applications of theories** you have studied. For example in business schools you will need to find up to date examples from the real world of business which you will analyse as applications of the theories you study, and in a course related to product design you can expect to design products with a specific function for a specific customer. As an example, one recent national student design competition was based around the changing needs of the UK population as it now has very many older people, therefore the students needed to design products with this particular group in mind. If you use an Internet search engine and the key words 'design student project' you will find a lot of interesting ideas for students studying courses in design which require them to apply their learning to solve specific problems. You will see much more about the need for application of theory in later in this book.

> **Learning tip** If you only repeat the theories (the *declarative* knowledge) and do not produce an analysis of a real-world situation (the *functional* knowledge), then you will not have demonstrated that you have achieved the intended learning outcomes. Spend several days analysing assessment instructions so you can understand exactly what is expected, and discuss your understanding of the task with other students. The instructions should clearly explain what the assessment is trying to measure, how you should present your work and how it will be marked.

Giving clear and prompt feedback

Another principle of assessment concerns feedback, in other words the comments teachers make after they mark your work. You should use the feedback from the teachers to feed forward to improve your future work; it is often said that we learn more from our mistakes than from our successes. Unfortunately – perhaps particularly if they are disappointed with the mark given for an assignment – often students quickly put away an assignment when it is returned and do not learn from the experience.

> **Learning tip** When you get your assignments back, carefully read the teacher's comments. If you are keeping a learning portfolio then change the comments into an action plan. For example the assignment brief above said the report needs to use the **Harvard referencing system**. If a student does not

do this correctly (see Chapter 11) they will lose marks and the teacher will comment on this. The student therefore needs to make a plan to ensure that in the future assignments marks will not be lost because of poor referencing.

Task 4.6   Getting feedback

For this task, show someone the summary you wrote earlier in this chapter about how you assess your own ability in different skills. This person does not have to be a teacher, it can be a friend or a classmate. First, ask them to comment on your ideas, your writing style and the accuracy of your language; and, then, rewrite the summary as a result of listening to this feedback.

Learning tip   It can be hard to listen to criticism, even constructive criticism. You should try hard not just to defend what you have done, and instead listen carefully (or read their comments carefully) to understand what the other person believes. Of course you may decide after thinking about it that you still do not want to change your position, but that position will now be clearer to you because you have looked at it from another point of view. This is part of developing critical awareness which you are building up throughout this course.

Different approaches to assessments

There are an enormous number of different types of assessment, and you will examine some examples of these at the end of the chapter. First though, we will look at several different general approaches which universities use, and this will help us to analyse the specific examples you will see later.

Individual assignments and group assignments

There are some assignments (such as examinations) which are always done by individuals, and some (such as the project about an organization's communications you saw earlier) which are most commonly done by groups. It is important that you see that these are assessing different skills. Group work should show that you have developed and used group working skills. In some group assignments you will need to keep minutes of the meetings you had, that is a record of the decisions you took and the responsibilities given to different team members. In a group presentation you will need to show that you have prepared and practised this together. The ability to work as a team will be part of the module's intended learning outcomes. The details will be set out in the assignment brief, and the marks allocated to demonstrate this will be specified in the marking scheme. When it is not possible to identify the individual contributions, for example if the group collectively create a report on their project, then usually all members will get the same mark; but sometimes a part of the total mark will also be given for individual work such as keeping a reflective log of the process.

Teacher assessment, self-assessment and peer assessment

Although it is most common for teachers to assess students' work, there are situations when you are asked to give your own work a mark, or to give marks for other students' work. To do this you will be given the marking scheme which allocates marks for the different components of the assignment, and then you will need to decide how well you (or your classmates) have done each part of the task. For the assignment you looked at earlier concerning branding and charities the marking scheme could be something like this:

- 20 percent: knowledge of theoretical concepts related to branding.
- 10 percent: review of research into charity branding.
- 10 percent: analysis of the case study charity methods of communication.
- 20 percent: quality of primary research.
- 20 percent: evidence of evaluation.
- 20 percent: quality of report presentation (IT skills, language, referencing).

Task 4.7   Pair work

In Task 4.3 there are some details concerning the requirements of a group assignment about an organization's communications (notice, however, that this is not the complete assignment brief). By examining this information discuss what marks you would give for each aspect. Notice that this task involves producing several different things: some individual, some as a group, some written and some spoken. You will need to make sure that each intended outcome has marks allocated to it, and that these total 100 percent.

Peer assessment refers to students giving marks to other students. This is often linked to some form of group work, for example a student led seminar which you will find out about later. This again will involve having a marking scheme and – as with self-assessment – the intention is to encourage you to focus on the intended outcomes of the assignment. For example if the instructions ask you to produce a case study, or to make five recommendations, or to compare two different types of organization, then recognizing that each part of the instructions has specific marks allocated to it will help you to keep on target.

Formative assessment and summative assessment

The word 'formative' is connected to the idea of something being developed or someone being trained, in other words the process is not yet finished, so **formative assessment** refers to finding out how you are progressing during a course. For example after a lecture the tutor may put a series of multiple choice questions on the VLE connected to the course. You can then complete this online test and get an instant mark to show you how much of the lecture you have properly understood. This will help you to identify which topics you need to read more about and, if lots of students misunderstand the same point, it helps the lecturer to see which topics need to be covered again. The marks from these formative assessments will not be counted as part of your overall mark for the course. The word 'summative' is connected to the idea of looking back, so **summative assessments** refer to any way of finally giving students marks, most crucially passing or failing a module or course. Using another example, in a course which is built around a series of student led seminars it is possible that the first time each group of students leads a seminar they will receive a formative mark along with comments from the tutor and the other students in the seminar group, and they can use this feedback to help them improve their performance. Then the second time they lead the seminar they will receive a summative mark, which is part of the course assessment.

Learning tip There is a danger of not treating formative assessments seriously, of thinking that they are not really important. You will see in Chapter 5 that an important theory of learning involves reflection – seeing learning as something which happens over a period of time, and that as we learn we change. Receiving feedback in any form assists in this process of change and reflection, so consider all feedback carefully.

Continuous assessment and end of course assessment

If in your previous education the most important form of assessment you have experienced has been end of year examinations you may assume that assessments always happen at the end of a course. You will find, however, that there are assessments at different times of the year: for example there may be an examination at the end of a module worth 40 percent of the total assessment, but you may also need to write an individual essay after two months of the course for another 20 percent, and to work with a group of students to design a web page two months after this for another 40 percent. You will complete a task about planning and preparing for **continuous assessment** in Chapter 6.

Task 4.8   Small group discussion

For these different approaches to assessment discuss what you think are possible advantages and disadvantages, also tell each other what has been your previous experience of assessments – have you used any of these approaches?

- Individual and group assignments.
- Teacher, self- and peer assessment.
- Formative and summative assessment.
- Continuous and **end of course assessment**.

Learning tip   Time management is a vital key skill, and remember you may be studying several different modules at the same time. Also each module may have two or three different assessments at different times of the year, so you will probably be working on several assessments at the same time, some individually, some with different groups of classmates. It is essential, therefore, that at the beginning of the year you read each module guide; identify what the assessments are going to be; note when they must be completed; and then make a plan of all assignments which you can put onto a year planner.

Types of assessment

The examples given here are not intended to be a complete list of the different types of assessments you will find but are a selection to give you an idea of the many kinds of assessments used. Some common forms of assessment like essays, portfolios and presentations are dealt with elsewhere in this book and so are not included here. Also remember that the examples given here are only brief summaries, and you will find that the assignment briefs for your assessments are usually much longer and more complex. Note that most of the written types of assignment expect an objective (impersonal) style of writing, but some use a subjective (personal) style. You will examine the differences between these styles in the next chapter.

Reports

Reports – unlike essays – are arranged with clear section headings, and when used in student assessments are often based on various professional formats related to the topic being studied. Indeed in certain vocational courses – such as degrees in nursing, education and social work – a part of being able to join the profession is knowing the expected format of reports used in that profession, and therefore you need to practise these while you are a student. It is important to use the exact format supplied for each report you are asked to do, and if the instructions do not make this expected format clear, then you must contact the tutor to enquire about it. You must aim for professional standards in your completed report, and normally these are written in an objective style. Earlier in this chapter there was an example where the required structure was: a title page; a contents page; an executive summary; theoretical background; the case study; your findings from primary research; your recommendations.

Literature reviews

Students need to read widely, use a range of different types of sources and expect that different writers will come to different conclusions concerning any one question. **Literature reviews** are assignments which encourage you to start doing these things. Often you may find a literature review as an assessment near the beginning of a course, but later on you may have longer assignments, such as a dissertation, which will contain a literature review as a part of it. Normally these are written in an objective style.

Example from a module concerning information systems

For this task you need to produce a 1000 word literature review concerning the increase in uses of social software in the twenty-first century. You should refer to at least eight different sources of information (including at least one book, one journal article, one website and one newspaper). Your review should not just be a list of summaries of the different texts but instead you should develop several themes, for example 'growth', 'diversification of uses' and 'diversification of users'. It will be best if you read your sources before you finalize the themes you will use to structure your review, and in the review each theme should contain a synthesis of ideas taken from several sources. You must critically evaluate these sources, for example commenting on the quality of the research each is based on. You need to use the Harvard referencing system and include a bibliography.

- 40 percent: selection of suitable sources.
- 40 percent: analysis, synthesis and evaluation of ideas.
- 20 percent: presentation of review (including referencing).

Case studies

You will be told again and again that one key feature of the assignments at university involve the application of theories to real-world situations. Case studies are very good examples of this approach. Sometimes you will be given case studies to analyse and sometimes you will need to select your own examples. The tasks will require you to demonstrate both a clear understanding of theory and to use these theories to solve problems related to the case study. Normally these are written in an objective style. In the following example the assignment is a case study which contains a literature review and the whole thing should be presented in a report format.

Example from a module concerning operations management

Read the case study documents which are on the module VLE, which concern the operations management situation in a food processing company. Pay particular attention to evidence concerning the costs the company is facing and reflect on how this affects the company's profitability. Write a report of the situation for the senior management of the company, and include these elements:

- A description of the situation which currently exists which clearly identifies the problems you have found.
- A literature review to find examples of good practice in similar companies/situations (expect to use more than five different sources).
- Recommendations for changes which will adapt good practice models to address this company's problems.

The assignment must be produced in the format of a professional report with an executive summary, a contents page, clearly labelled sections and it must conclude with a list of recommendations. It should be 2000 words long. You should also attach a reference list (Harvard referencing should be used).

- 30 percent: analysis of case study materials and identification of problems.
- 30 percent: literature review (selection of suitable sources, analysis of good practice).
- 20 percent: suitability of recommendations.
- 20 percent: presentation style and professionalism.

Dissertations

Often final year undergraduate students and most Masters' students need to write a dissertation. This, depending on your subject and level, may be between 10,000 and 20,000 words long. The dissertation involves a series of stages over several months: first, choose a topic related to the subject that you want to research; second, carry out a literature review to find out what is already known and published on this topic; third, design your own research methods (we will look briefly at primary research in Chapters 8 and 9); fourth, carry out the research for example by getting people to fill in a questionnaire;

fifth, analyse your findings; and, sixth, write up your dissertation. This is often the final step in getting a degree.

Web design and evaluation

You will see in Chapter 9 that students often need to obtain information from websites, particularly when you need up to date information, but also that you need to assess the quality of the websites you use very carefully.

Creating websites is also becoming an important skill, indeed, perhaps this may soon become as important as writing reports, and so it is a key skill related to communication. An effective website has information which is carefully selected, clearly presented and logically arranged. The information it contains should be as carefully researched as any other form of communication such as essays or articles.

Example from a module concerning physical geography

This assignment requires you to do the following:

1 Refer to the topics covered in weeks four–seven of the module to create a checklist of the things you need to consider when you evaluate a website for educational purposes.
2 Find three websites that relate to some aspect of geography, for example institution websites, business websites, educational websites and so on.
3 Critically evaluate these three websites using the checklist you have prepared.

(*50 per cent of total mark.*)

For the second part you must design an educational webpage yourself about: 'The Formation of the Earth and Moon'.

(*50 per cent of total mark.*)

The following learning outcomes and key skills will be assessed:

• Understanding and explaining the language of physical geography and geology.
• Demonstrating proficiency in the development of logical arguments by means of appropriately referenced written work.
• Demonstrating the ability to find and use information from a range of sources including fieldwork, library searches and Internet resources.
• Producing information in the form of a web page which is carefully selected, clearly presented and logically arranged.

Student led seminars

You saw in Chapter 2 that seminar discussions are essential in this method of learning, and you will see again later in this course that hearing a variety of answers and opinions is seen as a much deeper form of learning than finding and memorizing one 'correct' answer. On some modules students can be asked to lead a seminar (usually working in small groups) and the teacher observes and assesses the students, looking at the students leading the seminar and also at the participation of other students in the class. Usually near the beginning of the course there is a list of topics which is divided between the students (so for a seminar of 20 students they may form five groups of four students each) and each small group is given two topics. In the first seminar which they lead the students may get feedback and be given a formative mark, then later when they lead their second seminar they will receive a summative mark. To get a good mark you need to research the topic, give the seminar group an outline of the issues connected to it, prepare some form of whole class discussion (for example using a case study which you prepare) and then lead the discussion.

Example from a module concerning ethical business

The seminars will require you discuss an ethical question in a business situation. Your group needs to research the topic you have chosen and lead a seminar (20–25 minutes) including your introduction to the topic and a discussion which you will lead. Example of suitable topics:

- Advertising possibly dangerous products (for example tobacco).
- Using stereotype images in advertising (for example associating beautiful people, powerful people or famous people with a product).
- Outsourcing manufacturing to developing countries.

(*25 percent: evidence of research and preparation; 25 percent: introduction to topic; 50 percent: seminar activities and discussion.*)

---

e-Assessments

There are an increasing number of assessments linked to VLEs, and earlier in this chapter you saw that it is possible for the VLE to have formative questions covering the main topics of a lecture. These can be multiple choice or gap-fill questions which will be computer marked and give you instant feedback. Other assessments now use social software and encourage group working, so these can also be used on distance learning courses.

Examples of e-assessments

Wikis: when a group of students collectively edit and amend a document, for example the assignment you looked at earlier about investigating the methods of internal communication used in a company in order to write a report could make use of a Wiki. As an electronic text this could then have links to other texts on the Internet.

Blogs: these are individually produced, they are added to over time like a diary. Blogs can be used as an electronic version of the portfolios you have already considered, but they can also be published for others to read. An example taken from a literature module relating to children's books asked students to keep a blog during one semester adding one posting every month to give an analysis of six different children's books. In addition each student had to post feedback to at least six other students' blogs.

Examinations

You may think you are very familiar with examinations already, but you should be ready for different varieties, for example **open-book exams**, where you can take in some books and notes to refer to during the exam, and **time constrained test** where you have more time to prepare for a question which you must then answer in examination conditions.

Part Two

The study process

Introduction

In Chapter 2 you saw that universities are 'cultures of learning' and that the expectations of what students and teachers should do can be different in different places. In this part of the book you will explore the methods of studying which are commonly used in English speaking universities, to see what people in these universities believe knowledge actually is, and the things you will be expected to do as a student. The four chapters in this part of the book will take you through the stages which students follow each time they begin a new module or a new area of study.

The four chapters in this part are:

5 Starting out: what do I already know?
6 How can I understand my topic?
7 How do these ideas connect?
8 Group working: what do other people think?

Each chapter will explore related approaches, methods and skills.

- **Approaches**: these will outline the theories of learning and teaching associated with this stage of the learning process.
- **Methods**: these will describe the particular behaviours of students and teachers which arise from these approaches.
- **Skills**: these are exercises to develop the study skills (including language and personal skills) necessary for these methods.

5

Starting out: what do I already know?

Theme: development

Aims of this chapter

By the end of this chapter you will have:

- Explored what is meant by constructivist learning.
- Explored what is meant by the reflective approach to learning.
- Become familiar with using discussions as a method of learning.
- Become familiar with using portfolios as a method of learning.
- Practised the skills and language required for discussions.
- Practised the skills and language required for subjective and objective writing.

Introductory exercise: the aims of development

Consider these goals that the government of a developing country might have:

- Supplying clean water for all people.
- Creating jobs.
- Protecting the environment.
- Building schools.
- Building modern cities.
- Creating an infrastructure of roads and railways.
- Training doctors and nurses.
- Building up the size and strength of the army.

- Building hospitals.
- Starting new industries.
- Increasing exports.
- Improving agriculture.

Task 5.1   Examining your own beliefs

Select the five goals in the list above which you feel should have the highest priority. For each one you should make some notes to be ready to explain why you think this should be a priority. Put your notes in Part B of your portfolio.

Task 5.2   Small group discussion

If you are doing this course with a group of other students, compare your goals from the task above with a group of classmates; if you are following this course alone, then show your goals to some friends. Together discuss what you feel should be the priorities for development. Remember the important phrase: 'In my opinion . . .'.

Approach 1: Transmission versus constructivist learning

You have seen that every course that you will study will have clear intended learning outcomes (ILOs) and these will be described in your course and module guides. These ILOs may include some things such as key facts that you should remember and be able to explain (declarative knowledge) but usually the main focus is on knowing how to do things (functional knowledge). If you look back to the description of undergraduate courses you saw in Task 2.7 you will see that most of the techniques and skills described are about this kind of functional knowledge such as problem solving skills, effective communication and decision making. How, then, should you achieve these intended learning outcomes?

Education in English speaking universities is NOT based on an assumption that:

- Teachers know a lot.
- Students know little.
- Therefore teachers should transmit knowledge to students.
- Students should then repeat what they have learnt in examinations.

The assumption above is a **transmission model** of education which is not accepted in these universities. Instead of this expect what is often called constructivist learning.

Task 5.3   What do you think?

These are some of the key features of the *constructivist learning* model, read each point then mark with:

☑☑ = I strongly agree.
☑   = I agree.
☒   = I disagree.
☒☒ = I strongly disagree.

Students will often begin a course with existing ideas of the topic even if these are very vague, for example the tasks above (5.1 and 5.2) were asking you to use your existing ideas about the topic of development, even though you may not have studied development theory.   □

As you go through a course you are constantly connecting new ideas to your existing ideas on a topic, perhaps changing your ideas, perhaps seeing new ways of looking at them.   □

The student is therefore constructing her or his own understanding of the topic.   □

This understanding is often a result of interacting and talking with other people, so each person's understanding is constructed in social groups, it is not something we do on our own.   □

The task of the teachers is to create opportunities and give support for students so they can learn and find out for themselves, which is to create the opportunity for student centred learning.   □

Learning activities should therefore involve students discussing different ideas, looking at real-world problems and interactive group work.   □

The assessments should be intended to help both the learners and the teachers to see if the ILOs are being achieved.   □

The transmission model of learning assumes that knowledge is something that can be given by one person to another, as if it were a solid object. In contrast, in the constructivist model used in these universities, knowledge is not seen as being fixed in this way, knowledge is something which changes and grows, and different people will see any topic or situation differently. It is important for you to understand that just about everything you may study at university concerns this kind of knowledge. Remember the Learning tip from Chapter 2:

> **Learning tip**   When you are at university do not think about 'answering' questions, it is better to think about 'discussing' questions. Be prepared to find that there is almost never a single agreed answer to any question, but a range of different 'schools of thought' which you will need to evaluate. This idea of evaluation will be developed throughout this book.

This leads to the next important approach, which also sees knowledge as being something in constant change.

Approach 2: Reflective learning

This approach to learning goes beyond the idea that learning is about finding then remembering new facts and information. Reflection combines the idea of looking back in time with the idea of looking at ourselves, just as we look at our own reflection in a mirror.

This approach sees learning as a process which happens over a period of time, and that the new things we are learning may challenge our existing ideas on a topic, so as we learn we change. Reflection is about calmly looking back over a learning episode and thinking not just about what you have learnt, but also about the way you felt during the process of learning. Accepting new things can sometimes be difficult or can make you feel uncomfortable, because you may need to change your ideas about which things are true, which things are good, and which things you like. At other times as you reflect you may feel good, proud of your achievements and the new skills you have developed.

One of the major theorists often referred to in connection with reflective learning is Kolb (1984). His theory describes four learning styles, and different people prefer one of these styles. The styles are:

- Concrete experience: learning by doing.
- Reflective observation: thinking back over a learning experience.
- Abstract conceptualization: when we form a more general idea based on experience.
- Active experimentation: when we try out our ideas in new situations.

However, although people may prefer one particular style, the theory recognizes that all people go through a cycle of all four styles as they learn from experience, so we all reflect on previous experiences, then create 'abstract concepts' which we go on to test in future situations.

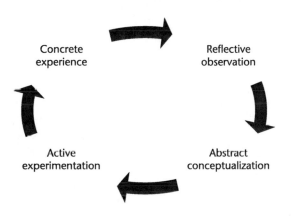

Figure 5.1 The learning cycle

Source: Based on Kolb, D. (1984) *Experiential Learning.* London: Prentice Hall International.

What do teachers say?

Dean of the graduate school:

Reflective learning enables students to investigate their strengths and weaknesses.

Principal lecturer in English:

Using reflective learning helps students to place each experience into the context of their whole lives.

Head of centre for work based learning:

To make the most of your experience you should take time to stand back, review the things you did and sort them into different skills, noting the skills you engaged in for the first time and the experiences that helped you develop existing skills.

Task 5.4 Pair work

Think about a learning experience you have had recently, it does not need to be in a school or university situation, it could be something like learning how to use a new computer programme, or a machine, or learning to drive, or doing a new job. Now talk about this experience with another student; use these questions to tell them:

- What happened.
- How you felt.

- What was successful.
- What was unsuccessful.
- What you will do in similar situations in the future.

Learning tip   Remember, a key idea of reflection is that you are not just looking at the topic you are studying but also at yourself: how you are changing, the difficulties you may be having and the achievements you are obtaining.

Method 1: Discussions

The first method of learning which results from the ideas of constructivist and reflective learning is the value universities place on discussions, for example in seminars. This was one of the key features of UK university education reported by international students in Chapter 2.

These are some features usually associated with discussion as a method of learning:

- Instead of giving students information the teacher creates a dialogue by asking questions. In universities this dialogue takes place in seminar discussions.
- We should begin the discussion with an open mind, ready to receive the ideas of others.
- We never fully and finally know something: we can always add to our ideas and change what we think as we get more ideas and information.
- Different people may understand a question differently, so the discussion often begins by discussing definitions of the key concepts of the topic.
- One result of discussion is that all the participants gain a clearer understanding by developing their own ideas: when we need to give ideas and examples to others we have to clarify what we think.
- Another benefit of discussion when we are learning a new language is that we notice that there are things we want to say that we cannot express clearly. This encourages us to learn.

Can you suggest more benefits of using discussions?

> **Learning tip** The use of seminar discussions is sometimes described as 'Socratic education'; this is because the philosopher Socrates used questions and answers as a method of teaching. The questions teachers ask to set off discussions are not questions looking for a single answer which is 'correct'; instead they are questions to create discussions and which expect to produce a range of different responses. To say 'I don't know' is not acceptable, the questions are not asking what you know, but what you think. Many teachers believe that the three most important words in education are: 'In my opinion . . .'.

What do students say?

Student from Switzerland:

It's fundamental, the communication, the discussion with people, knowing what other people are thinking. Today the level of business is international, so we are always working with different kinds of people, so it's necessary to know what they think.

Student from Brazil:

At the beginning we always think that we are right, that our point of view is the right one, but when we meet people from different cultures we see that in fact there is no right no wrong just different points of view. It's necessary to discuss with other people to understand them.

Student from China:

It's a really good learning style to see each other's ideas, to change ideas, most of us really enjoy this.

Student from Czech Republic:

It's like a debate you can say, the teacher tries to make a debate between students, it's not just teacher and student, he'll try to put in some arguments, so people will start talking and other people will have different views, they do encourage you to discuss things.

Method 2: Portfolios

Writing about our thoughts and feelings helps us through the changes which come with learning, and so many courses expect you to complete learning logs or portfolios. In the Introduction to this book you read about the need to complete a portfolio as you work through this book, and you saw that portfolios are a common method of assessment. It is a mistake, though, if you think a portfolio is only a method of assessment: a portfolio should be kept throughout the course first of all as a method of learning, then later as something that can be looked at for assessment.

Learning tip   To be a successful student it is necessary to engage with the course materials, to participate in all the activities such as researching, discussions, lectures and to read texts as directed. Therefore you must keep your portfolios up to date, particularly if you have several portfolios for different modules, and you should read through them as your courses progress to be aware of your own development.

Skill 1: Discussion skills

The first and most important discussion skill you must develop is the willingness to participate. If you only sit and listen then you are taking ideas from the others in the group without giving anything in return. When someone else has spoken, always say something – even if it's just, 'Yes, I see'. If you are usually reluctant to talk then set yourself a series of targets: to say more and more in each week's seminar.

The second skill you must develop is the ability to listen, not just to hear, as this helps you to be open-minded and to be willing to change your views. Listening means trying to understand other people's meanings, not just to hear their words.

The third skill is to develop your interpersonal relations, to see the discussion as a team working together to solve a problem; it is not a debate you are trying to win.

The following phrases are useful in discussions:

Language to break the ice:

- *Does everybody know each other?*
- *Has anybody got any ideas about this?*
- *What do you think?*
- *What's your opinion?*

Language to state opinions:

- *In my opinion . . .*
- *I think . . .*
- *My idea is . . .*

Language to agree:

- *Yes, that's a good idea.*
- *I think that's right.*
- *I agree with you (completely / up to a point).*
- *I see what you mean.*

Language to disagree:

- *I see what you mean, but perhaps . . .*
- *No, I don't agree with that . . .*
- *I'm sorry, but I see it differently . . .*

At the beginning of this chapter you took part in a group discussion about the topic of development, without studying any of the theories in this complex area. This was to demonstrate that we often have ideas about topics before we actually begin to study them. For the next task you will first read some online articles about different models of development and then you will do another group discussion exercise.

Online readings: development

On the website connected to this book www.openup.co.uk/international students there are two readings concerning development, and you will find one other yourself using an Internet search engine. Read through these three source texts online, but you should read them quite quickly just to get a general understanding. You will find out more about techniques for reading for general information like this in Chapter 6.

1   Oxfam (2008) *Livelihoods*. [online]. Oxford: Oxfam International. Copyright © Oxfam 2008.
2   For the second text you should use an Internet search engine and the key words 'Beyond Economic Growth'. You are searching for an online textbook with this title published online by the World Bank. When you find this you should read the first chapter entitled: 'What is development?'
3   Bird, K. (2008) The political economy of pro-poor growth. ODI Briefing Paper No. 35. http://www.odi.org.uk/resources/odi-publications/briefing-papers/35-political-economy-pro-poor-growth.pdf   Overseas Development Institute, London.

Task 5.5   Readings

Now read the descriptions of the three development schemes below. For each one, you should decide who you think will be the people who will benefit from the scheme, and if there are any major advantages or disadvantages to it.

Scheme one: island sugar scheme

All countries need foreign exchange, earned by exporting, in order to fund imports. This is an important priority for all developing countries, because they need to import so many essential things such as medicines and technology, and to pay the interest on previous borrowing. This scheme is in a Caribbean island country which needs to generate foreign exchange. The scheme proposes to compulsorily purchase land from a village of subsistence farmers, then to upgrade the land by levelling and supplying irrigation, and to use it for the growing of sugarcane ('compulsory purchase' is when the government forces the owners to sell). A sugar refinery will also be built to process the sugarcane into refined sugar for export. The farmers concerned are rather conservative, and they claim they are satisfied with their current income from growing and selling vegetables. These, however, are marketed locally and do not contribute to export earnings. The people in the village are not rich, but they have a comfortable basic life. The new scheme will provide employment – either in the fields or the refinery – for all those farmers who will be dispossessed, so no one will be unemployed. The life style of the village will change, but the country as a whole will benefit from the foreign exchange earned by the exports. The government of the island will jointly fund the project, paying all local costs, but they need aid from abroad for the purchase of imported equipment.

Scheme two: central African health centre

In this rural area of a central African country there is a population of 200,000 spread over a large area, mostly living in villages but with one town with a population of 40,000. The health centre in this town is in a bad state of repair, and this proposal is to replace it with a new building on a new site. Health statistics for the area reflect a low standard of health care. Infant mortality is high, due to low nutrition and a lack of clean water. There is a high level of Bilharzia, a disease which is spread by contact with infected water. In recent years HIV/AIDS has spread in the area and caused increasing poverty. In addition, for several years this area has been affected by drought, which has increased malnutrition and poverty. There has been a reduction in quality of life indicators, such as the percentage of children attending school, infant mortality and access to clean water. Increasing numbers of men are leaving their families to find work in the cities. Aid is needed for the construction of the new health centre and to finance the first six months' running costs.

Scheme three: valley women's education scheme

If you educate a man you educate an individual, if you educate a woman you educate a community. (Proverb)

Many problems related to development – family size, nutrition and agricultural production – are directly related to women. It has been shown in many previous projects that simple literacy schemes targeted directly at women have far-reaching effects. Even a small level of education empowers women to take more control of their lives, and this is shown in increased production and reduced family size.

This scheme is to set up a string of education centres in one of the poorest areas of a country in Asia. As well as building these centres it will finance a team of trainers skilled in numeracy, literacy and nutrition. The courses will be run in the evenings for women and girls who have had no formal education

Task 5.6   Group discussion

Work in groups of four or five students. You are the committee of a development charity and this meeting is to decide how to spend the money you have collected from public donations. You have raised enough money to fund only one of the three projects. You are going to discuss each project in turn, to identify the strengths and weaknesses of it. Then you will decide which one of the three you will give the money to. In the discussion practise the discussion skills and phrases described above: *participate, listen, work as a team.*

Skill 2: Objective and subjective writing

You may have been taught that academic writing should always be impersonal or objective, and this style of writing uses various ways of showing the focus is on the topic not the writer,

- By focusing on the topic.
- By using the passive voice.
- By using references to other people's ideas, and using introductory words for sources and quotations.
- By using verbs which continue the idea of debate *(. . . may mean . . . can become . . .)*
- By using long and complex sentences, and formal vocabulary.
- By organizing the text with linking words, as development of ideas is very important.

When you are doing reflective writing, however, you should try to make it personal and subjective, as the focus is not on the topic but on yourself and the changes you are experiencing. Look at the following suggestions:

- Use the first person pronoun as subject: *I, my, we, our.*
- Use verbs which focus on our thoughts, feelings or actions: *believe, know, feel, think, understand, mean, recommend.*
- Use personalized expressions: *it seems to me, it appears, from my point of view, in my view, in my opinion, as far as I can tell/see.*
- Use modal verbs like: *should, must, ought to, will.*
- Use signals of opinions like: *certainly, definitely, undoubtedly, clearly, obviously, fortunately, unfortunately, unhappily.*

Task 5.7   Pair work

In pairs, read these three extracts taken from the reflective logs of different students' portfolios. Can you find examples of:

- A student changing her or his opinion about something.
- A student reflecting on a lengthy process of learning.
- A student saying that s/he was surprised.
- A student describing how her or his approach to learning changed.
- A student reporting that s/he felt good about something.
- A student describing how s/he overcame a difficulty.
- A student saying that her or his ideas changed because of other points of view in a discussion.

Extract 1

This is an example of a student reflecting on a seminar she took part in where the students had been discussing whether Internet based companies (e-commerce) should keep personal information about customers.

> I changed my ideas through the seminar discussion. Before the seminar, I did think that IT service companies have a responsibility to protect the customers' personal information, and they cannot sell the information to the third party without permission, but I did not think that people really need to be afraid of their personal information being known. However, after the seminar, I certainly think now that people need to be careful about the personal information they give. The reason is that we do not know what will happen after using IT to do something . . . Therefore in my opinion IT corporations should be responsible when it concerns their customers' privacy information, and customers should be cautious themselves as well.

Extract 2

This is an example of a student reflecting on a session concerning referencing and **plagiarism**, both of which we will cover later in this book.

> The session taught us some things on referencing and how to structure an essay. I also learnt that surprisingly 10% of the whole marks can come from correct referencing so it was something we should watch out for. I was grateful for that piece of advice. I also learnt more about plagiarism which simply means to lift information from a book without giving the author and the publisher ... Another thing I learnt was about paragraphs. I knew that it was right to use paragraphs in essays but I never knew that it was such a big thing, from what I gathered putting paragraphs and making a piece of work structured could make the difference between getting a C and a B.

Extract 3

This is an example of a student reflecting on the process of doing group research to prepare a presentation; you will be doing something similar later in this book.

> The first time I heard that I was to do a group presentation there was a mix of emotions running through me. I was scared and excited to be carrying out my first presentation. The Wednesday we were given the assignment we arranged a group meeting in the library and fortunately we were all present at that first meeting. We divided the work equally among us. We had difficulties arranging to meet after that because we all worked on different days. One student was unfortunately hitting a dead end because she said she could find no theories ... When we did meet to practise one of the students could not come because she had to go to her embassy so we had to divide her part up ... One of the group made the PowerPoint, I thought there were too many animations and also it was too colourful so I gave my opinion to the group but the others seemed to think it was okay ... I really enjoyed working with my group members and the presentation was a wonderful experience.

Task 5.8   Portfolio task

At the beginning of this chapter you took part in a discussion about development, and later you read some articles and then took part in another discussion activity. For this Portfolio writing task you should describe how your thoughts about the topic may have changed as a result of both reading more and listening to other students' views. Remember that the focus of this writing is yourself, that is to say how your ideas concerning development may have changed; it is not an essay about development.

Employability link: key skills

You saw in Chapter 4 that in addition to the knowledge and skills directly related to the subject of your degree, the intended learning outcomes for many courses often include mention of developing key or **transferable skills**, which link your studies now to your future employability. Some courses also ask you to demonstrate more specific **information and communication technology (ICT)** skills.

Task 5.9

Can you do all of the following things using information and communication technology?

- Use word processing packages to write professional quality reports?
- Save and organize your own files?
- Work with email (using emails in a professional way rather than for chatting with friends)?
- Search for information on the Internet?
- Using software such as PowerPoint to give presentations?
- Use spreadsheets like Excel to present numerical information and to make graphs?

If you do not have these skills yet then make a specific plan about how you are going to develop them, as you will certainly need them to pass your degree (they will be ILOs for some courses) and you will need them in future jobs. Use the method of setting **SMART objectives** (specific, measurable, attainable, relevant, time-bound) and put your plan in Part A of your portfolio.

- *Specific*: Instead of just saying something vague – 'I will improve my word processing skills' – be much more exact: 'I will use word processing to keep a daily diary'.
- *Measurable*: Make the objective something you can measure: 'I will write 300 words each day'.
- *Attainable*: Don't make the targets too big as you may then get discouraged, hence 300 words a day, not 3000.
- *Relevant*: Make sure the skills are connected to your life and needs, for example if you will need to be able to design web pages then set this as an objective, don't try to learn skills which you will not be able to practise.
- *Time-bound*: When will each objective you set be finished?

Task 5.10 Critical incident discussion

Critical incidents are descriptions of situations where something has gone wrong, and from them it is possible to glimpse how inappropriate behaviours have resulted from cultural differences. Read through the following critical incident then discuss the questions below. Try to find more than one possible or acceptable answer to each question: the aim is not to find a 'correct' answer, but to see that different explanations are possible for any situation.

A student attends lectures and seminars regularly. The lectures are very useful, but s/he finds that the seminar discussions are often a waste of time because the teacher does not tell them anything new. Because s/he does not want to waste time in class she notes down the questions she wants to clarify, and approaches the teacher the end of the lesson to ask about these. At first the teacher seemed to like this, but recently has become evasive.

- What do you think this student expects to happen in the seminars?
- In your opinion why does the teacher begin to be evasive?
- Do you think this student has understood what the purpose of discussion is?
- What suggestions do you have to improve the situation?

Reference

Kolb, D. (1984) *Experiential Learning: Experience as the Source of Learning and Development.* London: Prentice Hall International.

6

How can I understand my topic?

Theme: corporate social responsibility

Aims of this chapter

By the end of this chapter you will have:

- Explored what is meant by being an autonomous learner.
- Explored the need for time management and planning.
- Become familiar with extensive reading.
- Become familiar with searching for information.
- Practised extensive reading skills: surveying, skimming, scanning.
- Practised note-taking strategies.

Introductory exercise: corporate social responsibility

The concept of corporate social responsibility (CSR) refers to a belief that companies should make sure that their activities do not damage the environment, or abuse their workers, and that their operations should support community and social development. There is a contrasting view, however, which is that companies exist to do business and do not have these social responsibilities. Instead they should only try to maximize their profits, and by doing this they will bring about the best situation for everyone: shareholders, customers and workers. Look at this example linking business with ethical behaviour:

On 28 October 2007 the *Observer* newspaper in the UK published a report concerning GAP, a highstreet fashion store. The report stated that factories making clothing in India for GAP stores in the UK were employing 10-year-old children in conditions close to slavery. This type of situation can happen when manufacturing is outsourced to another company, perhaps in another country, where it is not always easy to inspect what is happening. One part of the *Observer* report reads: 'According to one estimate, more than 20 per cent of India's economy is dependent on children, the equivalent of 55 million youngsters under 14'. This type of report can seriously damage a company like GAP, which spends vast amounts of money to build up its brand image, and does in fact have an ethical code it wants its suppliers to follow. It is an example of a company caught in the dilemma of wanting to appear responsible while still needing to operate with the lowest costs possible.

Task 6.1   Examining your own beliefs

First decide what you think about these ethical questions:

- Should companies worry about social, environmental, human rights issues?
- Should customers worry about the conditions of workers who make the things they buy?
- Should companies only make sure they obey the law or should they actually try to do good for society?
- Would you be willing to pay a higher price when shopping for clothes to be sure the workers are not being exploited?

Task 6.2   Small group discussion

Compare your ideas with a group of classmates or friends. Together discuss what you feel about this topic of corporate social responsibility. Notice that these questions are not asking for answers, they are asking for opinions, and they expect that different people will have different views.

Learning tip   Notice that the GAP example is a real-world case connected to the theory of corporate social responsibility, which all students in a business school study. You will see later in this book that most assignments will require this type of application of theory in practice, so you always need to follow the news regularly in order to collect examples of topics you are studying.

Approach 1: Extensive reading

You have seen in the previous chapter that the constructivist approach to learning assumes students already have ideas on most topics, and then as they find out more about a topic their ideas will constantly be changing. You have also seen that students are expected to spend most of their time reading to find these new ideas. A student beginning a new topic therefore needs to begin by reading widely, and using a range of different books and articles, written by different authors, to get a general idea of the topic. This chapter will concentrate on this type of quick, general reading (sometimes known as **reading for gist**) rather than deeper intensive reading which will be examined in Chapter 9.

Task 6.3   Discussion in pairs

Why do universities expect students to read different books on the same topic, written by different authors? Why should you not get one textbook and learn from that? What is your opinion about this?

When you begin to study a new topic you are entering a discussion which has been going on for many years. For example if you are going to study economics then this is a subject which goes back at least to the period of growing worldwide commerce in the seventeenth century, and the first writings about how markets work and why nations trade with each other. Some of the ideas of the early economists such as David Hume and Adam Smith, who wrote *An Inquiry into the Nature and Causes of the Wealth of Nations* in 1776, are still discussed by economists today. The principles of laissez faire economics; the division of labour; the role of government intervention; the advantages of trade – all these are topics which have been in the ongoing discussion which is the subject of economics for hundreds of years. Later on, other important thinkers were Thomas Malthus, David Ricardo and Karl Marx, and their ideas are still referred to in economics books and articles today. In the second half of the twentieth century a fierce debate emerged between two groups of economists – Keynesians and Monetarists – influenced by John Maynard Keynes and Milton Friedman respectively, and indeed this debate still continues now. Interestingly, Friedman is also the economist most connected with the view outlined earlier that companies should not attempt to demonstrate corporate social responsibility. He published an influential article 'The Social Responsibility of Business is to Increase its Profits' in *The New York Times Magazine* in 1970, and any student of this topic would need to read this article.

Learning tip There is a danger, particularly if you are studying in a foreign language, of trying to read everything intensively and deeply. There will be times when deep intensive reading is necessary, and you will look at this in Chapter 9, but in this chapter the skills you will develop are to get broad and general ideas by rapidly reading a large number of texts.

Task 6.4   Group discussion

What do you think are the origins of the following subjects, how long do you think they have been studied, do you know any of the key thinkers in them?

- Philosophy.
- Medicine.
- Computing.
- Psychology.

Make notes about the development of one of these topics and include the notes in Part B of your portfolio.

Approach 2: Learning involves ongoing autonomous discovery

You saw in the previous chapter that English speaking universities do not use an approach of transmission of information from teachers to students, and you explored the approaches of constructivism and reflective learning. A related approach – also central to this idea of how people should learn in this situation – is a belief in *autonomous learning* (also known as discovery learning), which means that students are expected to find things out for themselves. All of these theories demand that you are active in your learning, rather than just passively receiving ideas from your teachers. Your modules will supply indicative reading lists, perhaps even a week by week list of articles and chapters in books related to each week's lecture topic, but you will be expected to go beyond that, to find other texts and real world applications to show that you are an autonomous learner.

Task 6.5

These are some of the key features of the autonomous learning model, read each point then mark with:

☑☑ = I strongly agree

☑ = I agree

☒ = I disagree

☒☒ = I strongly disagree

> To be autonomous means to act for yourself, so an autonomous learner is someone who controls his or her own learning.　☐
>
> Students who find out things for themselves learn more deeply than students who are given information.　☐
>
> It is better not to have a single book which a course is studying, but instead to have lots of references for students to follow up.　☐
>
> It is better to have fewer hours of taught lectures and lessons so you have more time to spend finding information in the library or on the Internet.　☐
>
> Teachers should suggest things for students to find out, instead of telling you things to learn.　☐
>
> If students are autonomous they take more control of their learning, and the things they should learn, this is better than being told what to learn by teachers.　☐
>
> Autonomous learners need to be good at managing their time.　☐

> **Learning tip**　Often teachers use the word 'research' to describe this need for students to find information and examples themselves. You should be careful of the word 'research', however, as it can be used in different ways. The meaning of research here is just that you should not only rely on lectures and tutor's notes to build up your knowledge, instead you need to become an autonomous learner and find things out yourself by reading widely on the topics you are studying. Other meanings of research are to create new data for analysis, for example by designing a questionnaire survey or conducting interviews (primary research), or to process published data which you find, for example analysing a company's stock market valuations for a period of time (**secondary research**). You will find out more about these types of researching in Chapter 8.

The autonomous learner

- You need to multitask – to juggle the requirements of the different modules.
- You need to plan your use of time.
- You need to work on different types of assignments at the same time.
- You need to fit this into your full social life which was described in Chapter 3.

What do teachers say?

Professor of education:

> Autonomous learning is based on an idea of a Russian psychologist who suggested that what learners do with others today they will be able to do on their own tomorrow. The idea is that we want people to be as independent as possible, although we never become fully independent as we will always need to rely on other people for information we don't have. Effective learners are people who have opinions which have been shaped through experience and readings, but can synthesize the work of other people and see how it may change their opinions and views. They are people who have learned how to ask the right questions, by looking at information, taking details, taking facts, then analysing all of this and looking at the information again and forming critical questions.

Method 1: Finding texts for extensive reading

You should try using the following strategies to find books and articles so you can do the necessary amount of extensive reading at the beginning of a course.

- Look at any materials you are given connected to your courses, such as module guides – these should contain the indicative readings.
- Follow up any references made in lectures.
- If there is a VLE for your modules then check it regularly; tutors often put links to resources connected to the course on the VLE.
- During your induction period at the university you should attend any training sessions run by the library or IT services department; in particular you must learn how to use the library catalogue.
- Constantly try to improve your skills in using Internet search engines: it is easy to use them badly and find millions of useless hits, it is much harder to use them effectively to find a small number of hits which are related to your needs.
- Find your university library web pages: they will certainly have information and online tutorials on topics such as choosing keywords for searching and accessing databases.
- Follow the news daily, using good quality newspapers which have online editions such as:
  - *Guardian* at http://www.guardian.co.uk/
  - *The Times* at http://www.timesonline.co.uk/tol/news/
  - *Independent* at http://www.independent.co.uk/

> **Learning tip**   The key advice at this early stage of getting to know any new topic is:
>
> * It is better to read several articles quickly rather than one slowly.
> * It is important not to lose your confidence when you come across new terms – if you persist in your reading you will build up your knowledge of these terms and the concepts they refer to.
> * It is essential to note down the sources you use so that you will be able to reference them correctly later.
> * It is vital to keep up to date with the readings required by all your modules, for example the readings before seminars.

Method 2: Time management and planning

You have seen that new students may find that they are freer to decide how to use their time than they were earlier on in their education. Remember the examples of students' life styles you saw in Chapter 3: you may be living away from the university; you may find you have fewer contact hours with teachers than you are used to; and on some days you may have no lectures or seminars at all. On the other hand you may find you have a lot of demands on your time: you may have a part time job; you may need to cook your own food; and you will want to explore life and society in your new situation. It is essential, therefore, that you plan and manage your time because at the beginning of a course you will need to do the researching and extensive reading for each one of the modules you are studying, and then later in the course you will need to begin preparing the assignments for each of these. In some modules you may have continuous assessments such as portfolios which you must keep up to date each week throughout the course.

Task 6.6   Pair work

In this task you are going to make a study plan for a student for an 11-week term. Look at her diary and notice there are already some fixed items:

* She has lectures and seminars at the university on Monday mornings and afternoons; Wednesday mornings; and Thursday afternoons.
* She works in a supermarket on Thursday and Friday evenings and Saturday mornings and afternoons.

She is entitled to take 20 hours of paid leave from the supermarket at some time during this period, but she needs to book the leave days very quickly, so she needs to think about this as she makes her plan. Look at the list of things she has to do for her six modules (A–F) and then try to plan when she should do these things, and when she should take her holiday from the supermarket job. Put everything into her diary: her weekly reading time for each module; her preparation for assignments; the field trip; and her social and voluntary activities.

Mon 9–16 Uni	Tue	Wed 10–13 Uni	Thu 14–17 Uni 18–22 Supermarket	Fri 18–22 Supermarket	Sat 8–16 Supermarket	Sun
Mon 9–16 Uni	Tue	Wed 10–13 Uni	Thu 14–17 Uni 18–22 Supermarket	Fri 18–22 Supermarket	Sat 8–16 Supermarket	Sun
Mon 9–16 Uni	Tue	Wed 10–13 Uni	Thu 14–17 Uni 18–22 Supermarket	Fri 18–22 Supermarket	Sat 8–16 Supermarket	Sun
Mon 9–16 Uni	Tue	Wed 10–13 Uni	Thu 14–17 Uni 18–22 Supermarket	Fri 18–22 Supermarket	Sat 8–16 Supermarket	Sun
Mon 9–16 Uni	Tue	Wed 10–13 Uni	Thu 14–17 Uni 18–22 Supermarket	Fri 18–22 Supermarket	Sat 8–16 Supermarket	Sun
Mon 9–16 Uni	Tue	Wed 10–13 Uni	Thu 14–17 Uni 18–22 Supermarket	Fri 18–22 Supermarket	Sat 8–16 Supermarket	Sun
Mon 9–16 Uni	Tue	Wed 10–13 Uni	Thu 14–17 Uni 18–22 Supermarket	Fri 18–22 Supermarket	Sat 8–16 Supermarket	Sun
Mon 9–16 Uni	Tue	Wed 10–13 Uni	Thu 14–17 Uni 18–22 Supermarket	Fri 18–22 Supermarket	Sat 8–16 Supermarket	Sun
Mon 9–16 Uni	Tue	Wed 10–13 Uni	Thu 14–17 Uni 18–22 Supermarket	Fri 18–22 Supermarket	Sat 8–16 Supermarket	Sun

Mon 9–16 Uni	Tue	Wed 10–13 Uni	Thu 14–17 Uni 18–22 Supermarket	Fri 18–22 Supermarket	Sat 8–16 Supermarket	Sun
Mon 9–16 Uni	Tue	Wed 10–13 Uni	Thu 14–17 Uni 18–22 Supermarket	Fri 18–22 Supermarket	Sat 8–16 Supermarket	Sun

Module A: For this module she is keeping a portfolio, which takes one hour to write every week. She also needs to do about three hours of reading before the lecture on Wednesday morning.

Module B: For this module she is working on a group project. Each week she needs to research for about three hours, and she needs to arrange two meetings with her group which should each take about two hours: the first in the sixth week to discuss progress; the second in the ninth week to prepare and practise the presentation. It will be best to have these meetings after the module seminars on Mondays.

Module C: In this module she needs to go on a field trip with her seminar group to another town from Friday morning till Sunday afternoon at the end of the third week. She will then need to spend around 20 hours to write a report which must be handed in at the end of the seventh week.

Module D: For most weeks she needs to spend about four hours doing the weekly readings, however there will be an examination in the ninth week (on Thursday afternoon) so she hopes to spend about 20 hours revising just before this.

Module E: This is a modern language module (Italian), and the seminars are on Monday morning. Every week she needs to do some online exercises which take about two hours and must be submitted before midday on Friday (this is part of the module's continuous assessment).

Module F: She needs to hand in a 2500 word essay for this marketing module on the last day of the term. She cannot start until the end of the sixth week when the detailed instructions will be given. She expects to spend about 20 hours reviewing different theories, then 20 hours to research a real-world example case study, then 20 hours to write the essay.

Social activities: She also wants to play tennis twice every week, and to visit her boyfriend at a university in another town on at least two Sundays a month.

Volunteering: She would also like to help at a local school homework club from 3–4.30 on either Tuesdays or Wednesdays.

Online readings: corporate social responsibility

At the beginning of this chapter you looked at an example linking business to ethical behaviour, and began to think about the topic of corporate social responsibility (CSR). For the skills section of this chapter you will use some online readings on this topic to develop extensive reading skills. On the website connected to this book www.openup.co.uk/internationalstudents there are two readings concerning CSR, and you will find one other yourself using an Internet search engine.

1   Chryssides, G. and Kaler, J. (1996) *Essentials of Business Ethics*. Maidenhead: McGraw-Hill. (Section on 'Five views of business ethics', pages 7–10).
2   Steiner, G. A. and Steiner, J. F. (2000) *Business, Government, and Society: A Managerial Perspective. Text and Cases*, 9th edn. Boston, MA: Irwin/McGraw-Hill. (Section on 'General principles of corporate social responsibility', pages 132–3).
3   Use an Internet search engine and the key words 'corporate social responsibility mission statement'; you are searching to find some examples of the policies of famous companies concerning this topic, for example you could use Starbucks, BP or Tesco.

Task 6.7   Readings

The second of these readings is reproduced here, and you will use this to practise the different reading skills. You will then use the other online texts to practise the skills for yourself. Do not try to read these articles deeply now, instead go directly to the skills exercises which will introduce ways of quick reading.

General principles of corporate social responsibility

No universal standard for social responsibility exists; managers must think carefully about what their companies need to do. The following are six general principles to guide them.

First, all firms must comply with two bodies of law: one is the body of corporation law that creates a fiduciary duty toward shareholders; the other is the body of regulation that protects all other stakeholders. Beyond this, there is no one formula for all business or a single business; often, situations are unique. In Colombia, the government gave Occidental Petroleum the legal right to explore in a remote area, but U'wa Indians claimed that drilling would defile sacred ground. Five thousand U'was threatened to commit collective suicide if Occidental went ahead. Occidental executives were unsettled by tribal history, which records a mass suicide to protest Spanish colonization in the seventeenth century. Each firm must decide for itself what it will and will not do. So far, Occidental has not moved into U'wa territory.

Second, corporations are economic institutions with strong profit motives; they should be judged primarily by economic criteria. They should not be expected to meet noneconomic objectives in a major way without financial incentives. As the Business Roundtable says in its *Statement on Corporate Responsibility*: 'If the bottom line is a minus, there is no plus for society. Companies may responsibly incur substantial short-run costs to correct social problems that threaten long-term profitability. And they may be encouraged to make profits by solving social problems'.

Third, corporations have a duty to correct the adverse social impacts they cause. Without this duty the exercise of corporate power is illegitimate. For example, a corporation should try to internalize *external costs*, or costs of production borne by society. A factory dumping toxic effluent into a stream creates costs – perhaps human and animal disease, perhaps the destruction of natural beauty – borne by innocents, not by the company or its customers. Corporations should not 'maximize' profits by imposing external costs, but should seek to reduce these costs.

Fourth, social responsibility varies with company characteristics such as size, industry, strategies, marketing techniques, locations, internal cultures, stakeholder demands, and managerial values. Thus, a global chemical manufacturer has a much different impact on society than a small, local insurance company, and its social responsibilities are both different and greater. Responsibilities also vary with national problems. A survey of 12,000 managers in twenty-five countries revealed great national variations concerning the priority managers give to different social issues.

Fifth, managers should try to meet the legitimate needs of stakeholders. Managers generally agree that their primary responsibilities are to five groups, which may be called dominant stakeholders: customers, stockholders, employees, governments, and communities. Managers often express their responsibilities to these groups in statements of corporate philosophy or, as they are also called, mission statements or credos. A well-known example is the credo of Johnson & Johnson shown on the following page. This credo is chiselled in stone at corporate headquarters.

However, as noted in Chapter 1, there are many other stakeholders, some of whom may from time to time become dominant. For example, when a firm is heavily in debt, the financial community and creditors may take the forefront. For a large corporation there are many stakeholders whose multiple demands conflict and cannot be completely met. So each company must set priorities to determine where, within its limited resources, it will meet legitimate demands.

Research suggests that the effort made by companies to respond to these primary stakeholders varies significantly among firms and between industries.

Sixth, managers can be guided by the general direction of a nation's public policy. Lee Preston and James Post believe that managers should follow a 'principle of public responsibility'; that is, they should figure out responsibility by studying the overall 'framework' of public policy, which includes 'not only the literal text of the law and regulation, but also the broad pattern of social direction reflected in public opinion, emerging issues, formal legal requirements, and enforcement or implementation practices.

(Steiner, G. A. and Steiner J. F. (2000) *Business, Government, and Society: A Managerial Perspective*, 9th edn. Boston, MA: Irwin/McGraw-Hill, pp. 132–3.)

Skill 1: Skimming and surveying

You should remember that the aim of the extensive reading skills presented in this chapter is not to get a deep understanding of each text by slowly understanding each and every word of it. Instead, the aim is to get a general idea of the many different aspects of a topic so that later you can use these general ideas in order to study the topic more deeply.

The first of these reading skills is '**skimming**' which involves:

- Looking over a document very rapidly just to get a general idea of what it is about and how it is organized.
- Often skim reading is connected with making decisions, for example if you are looking at a magazine in a bookshop and deciding if you will buy it, or if you are in a university library looking at a book and deciding if it is going to be useful for your assignment.
- When you look through a page of a newspaper you will skim through the different headlines to decide which articles interest you.
- There is a danger that when we read in a foreign language we will try to read everything too deeply. In our own first language we naturally skim read lots of things.

One good method of skimming is called '**surveying**', which means that you do not look at every word of a text or article. For example you may read only the introduction and then the first sentence of each of the other paragraphs. Using this method with the text above you would just read the following:

No universal standard for social responsibility exists; managers must think carefully about what their companies need to do. The following are six general principles to guide them.

First, all firms must comply with two bodies of law: one is the body of corporation law that creates a fiduciary duty toward shareholders; the other is the body of regulation that protects all other stakeholders . . .

Second, corporations are economic institutions with strong profit motives; they should be judged primarily by economic criteria . . .

Third, corporations have a duty to correct the adverse social impacts they cause . . .

Fourth, social responsibility varies with company characteristics such as size, industry, strategies, marketing techniques, locations, internal cultures, stakeholder demands, and managerial values . . .

Fifth, managers should try to meet the legitimate needs of stakeholders . . .

Sixth, managers can be guided by the general direction of a nation's public policy.

When you are surveying or skimming like this you should not stop to look up every word or idea you do not understand, but you may notice that there is a key concept which you want to check. In the above survey the concept of 'stakeholders' is used several times, so you might decide you need to look this up before continuing. In the next chapter you will look more deeply at using glossaries rather than dictionaries to build up your knowledge of subject specific concepts, but here is an example of looking up 'stakeholders' in a glossary.

• Step one: a student used an Internet search engine and the key words 'Glossary CSR', and found several online glossaries about corporate social responsibility.
• Step two: the student then selected one, a glossary produced by a project concerning social responsibility in small and medium-sized enterprises, available at:
  http://www.cecoa.pt/apoio/CSR%20Glossary_%20by_Subjects.doc
• Step three: this is the definition of 'stakeholder' that the student found in that glossary:

  An individual, community or organisation that affects or is affected by some aspect of an organisation's products, operations, markets, industries, and outcomes.

  Comment: stakeholders may be internal (for example, employees) or external (for example, customers, suppliers, shareholders, financiers, trade unions, ONGs, the media, the government or the local community).

(Cecoa 2004)

Task 6.8 Surveying exercise

Use the first online reading (Chryssides and Kaler 1996) to practice surveying: this time read only the introduction and the first paragraph (rather than the first sentence) of each of the 'five views' the authors mention. There may well be words that you do not recognize, and views you do not really understand deeply at this stage, but do not slow down or stop reading, just concentrate on the things you do understand. As you read ask yourself which of these views you now think makes the best argument, and whether your opinion on this topic has changed since the first task at the beginning of this chapter.

Learning tip It is important that you practise these fast reading skills, and to keep confidence even when you know that for the moment you are only taking in a small part of the texts. Remember the texts you will read are difficult; this is university level study! Do not expect to understand everything quickly, and do not panic when you have read something and think you have understood little in it.

Skill 2: Scanning

Another fast reading skill is '**scanning**' which involves:

- Looking through a document in order to find a specific piece of information, for example looking for one specific name in a list of names (often using a finger as well as your eyes).
- This is the way we read when we look up words in a dictionary, or look for information on a train or bus timetable.
- When you do this you actually give an instruction to your brain not to notice anything other than the item you are specifically looking for.
- You will often use scan reading when looking for specific information, for example finding statistics within an article.

Task 6.9 Scanning exercise

Scan through the article 'General principles of corporate social responsibility' (using your finger as well as your eyes) to find this information:

- There is a quotation from the Business Roundtable: what is it?
- Who has the greater social responsibility: a global chemical company or a local insurance company?

- How many managers were surveyed, in how many countries?
- Who are the dominant stakeholders mentioned?

Skill 3: Note taking

Later in this book you will look more deeply at note taking skills and the process of preparing assignments, but for the moment remember these points about assignments:

- In every assignment you will need to demonstrate that you have read widely on the topic.
- In every assignment you will need to demonstrate that you have examined different viewpoints on the topic.
- In every assignment you will need to demonstrate that you have been an autonomous learner and found extra sources of information about the topic.
- You will also normally need to examine applications of theory in practice.
- Therefore every student assignment should contain lots of references to the books and article you have read.

In Chapter 11 you will look in detail at how to do referencing correctly before you hand in assignments, but the following points concerning note-taking are important from the very beginning of a module:

- You do not want to waste any of the reading you have done, even the general background you do at the beginning of a module.
- Therefore you want to take something from every text you read, so that you can give this text as a reference and make your reference list as long as possible and demonstrate your extensive reading.
- The things you may want to take from this general type of reading include:
  - Definitions – usually any assignment will need definitions of key terms, probably near the beginning of the assignment.
  - Statistics – particularly up to date statistics from reliable sources.
  - Real-world examples of the theory in practice.
- Therefore you should take notes of definitions, statistics and examples you find in your reading, but as you may not be writing the assignment until several months later make sure that the notes are clear, and do not use loose pieces of paper as these may get lost.
- Similarly if you make notes on your PC or laptop, make sure you make back-ups.

> **Learning tip** You should make it clear if the notes are your own words or if you have copied an extract from the original. Note down all the information you will need later to include in the reference list/bibliography, these include: author name and initials; year of publication; title of book, article or journal; publishing details of books (city and name of publisher); volume number and issue number of journals; page numbers.

Task 6.10   Second reading and note taking exercise

You have already used quick reading techniques to skim two of the online readings related to this chapter, you have seen a real-world example concerning corporate social responsibility, and you have taken part in discussions. Now read these two articles again and look again at the examples you found of companies' CSR policy. This time, because you now have more background knowledge about the topic and have reflected more on it, you will probably find it easier to read the complete articles. Still, though, try to read as quickly as possible and do not worry about any words or sections you do not understand. From each article make notes about just one idea which you would later be able to use in a student's assignment. Put these notes in Part B of your portfolio.

Task 6.11   Portfolio task

Now look again at the four questions you considered at the beginning of this chapter. As a result of reading and reflecting have your views changed? Write around 100 words to outline your views on each of these questions, and include this in Part A of your portfolio):

- Should companies worry about social, environmental, human rights issues?
- Should customers worry about the conditions of workers who make the things they buy?
- Should companies only make sure they obey the law, or should they actually try to do good for society?
- Would you be willing to pay a higher price when shopping for clothes to be sure the workers are not being exploited?

Employability link: reflective learning and professional portfolios

The reflective learning approach does not just belong to education but also to your ongoing professional development. You may need to keep two types of portfolios: those which are connected to specific modules or courses where the portfolio becomes a product to be assessed and a **personal development portfolio (PDP)** which you build up over years (your whole career). You may be given a space on your university VLE to build up your own personal development e-portfolio. In this you should collect evidence to demonstrate how you are developing your skills and competences, and also you can use it to reflect on your achievements and experiences. One advantage of e-portfolios is you can access them from anywhere, another is that you can adapt the materials you have gathered for different uses: assessments; job applications; and your own personal reflection. This type of portfolio records your personal journey through life, it is never complete, and it is always open to change.

Learning tip   Do not just include evidence of your formal learning but collect other examples which are evidence of your skills. Here is an example: a student doing a work placement needed to collect evidence of his inter-personal communication skills for his work experience portfolio. English was not his first language but in the supermarket where he did his placement he had to deal with customers every day and, in particular, to respond to complaints. In one particular incident he successfully handled one very irate customer: listening carefully to what the complaint was about, responding appropriately and then recording the incident. Following this he asked a colleague to write a brief summary of what had happened and included this report as evidence in his work experience portfolio. He also kept the report in his personal development portfolio, so later he was able to use this as an example in an interview for another job, using it as evidence of his communication skills.

Task 6.12   Internet research

Use an Internet search engine and enter the key words 'continuing professional development + (profession)' for example 'continuing professional development accounting'; 'continuing professional development health care'; 'continuing professional development construction'. You will then find examples of how this concept is being developed in this profession. Although you may only be beginning your university career you should already be thinking about your future employment (remember what the careers adviser said in Chapter 2), so you need to begin preparing for your chosen profession now.

Task 6.13   Critical incident discussion

Critical incidents are descriptions of situations where something has gone wrong, and from them it is possible to glimpse how inappropriate behaviours have resulted from cultural differences. Read through the following critical incident then discuss the questions below. Try to find more than one possible or acceptable answer to each question: the aim is not to find a 'correct' answer, but to see that different explanations are possible for any situation.

A student on a Masters' course who is beginning a module on a new topic (international trade) has been told to do some extensive reading to get the feel of the topic. The student finds a book with the title *The Theory of Trade*, and reads it carefully, translating several sections of it into his own language to understand it exactly, and memorizing the important parts.

- Can you think of some positive aspects of what this student is doing?
- Can you think of some negative aspects of what this student is doing?
- In what ways has the student misunderstood the directions he has been given?
- What suggestions do you have to improve the situation?

7

How do these ideas connect?

Theme: eco-tourism

Aims of this chapter

By the end of this chapter you will have:

- Explored the first levels of a key theory of learning (Bloom's Taxonomy).
- Explored the importance of connecting ideas from different sources.
- Become familiar with using **figures** as a way to connect ideas.
- Become familiar with ways to put into your own words the ideas taken from research.
- Practised the skills of taking notes, from lectures and reading.
- Practised the language skills needed to connect ideas.
- Practised the skills of writing **paraphrases** and **summaries**.

Introductory exercise: eco-tourism

Tourism is rapidly becoming one of the major industries in the world, but tourism has a growing impact on the environment and people's lives, particularly in areas which rely heavily on tourist income. Consider how tourism affects the environment and people's lives by doing Task 7.1.

Task 7.1 Examining your own experiences

First, you should think about a holiday or trip you have taken yourself recently. It may have been in your own country or abroad, and it may have been just for one day or for a longer period. Think about the following questions:

- Did your holiday help the economic growth of the place which you visited?
- Did your holiday help to create employment?
- Who gained from any money you spent; were they local people, national companies, or international companies?
- What resources did you use on your holiday; think of things like roads, water, or energy?
- Do the facilities created for tourists in the place which you visited help to improve the local environment?
- Do the facilities created for tourists in the place which you visited help to improve the day to day life of local people?
- Do the tourist facilities in the place which you visited damage the local environment?
- Does tourism have any impact on the culture of the place which you visited, and is this impact positive or negative?

Task 7.2   Small group discussion

If you are doing this course with a group of other students then compare your experiences with some classmates, on the other hand if you are following this course alone then discuss the questions above with a friend.

Task 7.3   Discussion in pairs

In Chapter 6 you saw that a key concept related to corporate social responsibility was the need to identify the stakeholders in any activity. Now discuss with some other students or your friends who you think are the principle stakeholders related to the tourism industry. Make a list of who these people are. Put this list in Part B of your portfolio.

Learning tip   Notice that Task 7.3 asks you to take a concept from a topic you saw in a previous chapter and then to use it in connection with something different. Always try to do this, for example you saw in Chapter 2 that a student on a marketing course will study modules on different aspects of marketing, business studies and even accounting, but although these are different modules they are all contributing to developing the student's general understanding. You should always try to transfer ideas and skills you learn in one topic to other topics and modules.

Approach 1: Bloom's taxonomy

You have already seen that a necessary part of studying involves collecting ideas, theories, examples, definitions, statistics and so on from a variety of sources. Unfortunately some student assignments remain little more than a collection of extracts they have taken (**copy and paste**) from articles they have read. Their assignments, therefore, will get very low marks, and you will also see in Chapter 11 that reproducing ideas like this can be seen as plagiarism and can cause you to fail. In universities if a student just reproduces what other people have said or found then this is seen as the very lowest level of learning. One of the most influential theories concerning this approach to learning was produced by Benjamin Bloom and his colleagues in 1956. This provided a description of different levels of learning. In this **taxonomy** (which means a scheme of classification) there are six 'levels'. Figure 7.1 provides a description of the taxonomy beginning from the bottom (lowest) level **knowledge**.

University assignments are intended to allow students to show learning at the top end of this taxonomy. For example they usually require you to analyse and compare different theoretical approaches, to demonstrate applications in real-world situations (for example by researching how one

---

HIGHEST LEVEL

Evaluation: this means that you can make a decision concerning how you value the end-product of the information you have learned, for example you can compare different models or theories and decide which is best for a certain situation.

Synthesis: this means that you can combine and connect the ideas and information you have learned and use them in new contexts. Synthesis has the idea of connecting ideas and building up something new and original.

Analysis: this means that you can break down the information you have learned, to see how the ideas are organized, for example to understand causes of a situation or conclusions which come from it.

Application: this means that you can use the information you have learned in real world situations, to solve problems.

Comprehension: this means that you can demonstrate your understanding of what you have learnt.

Knowledge: this means that you can remember and repeat things you have learnt.

LOWEST LEVEL

Figure 7.1 Bloom's taxonomy

hospital manages communications with patients, or how a school is using theories from psychology to improve students' motivation for learning, or how a company plans to improve the efficiency of its supply chain, and so on). They usually require you to make a decision, for example to make recommendations. This book shows you how to push your work up to the highest levels, and so how to get the highest marks. In this chapter we will first concentrate on the two lowest levels, then the two middle levels will be discussed in Chapter 9, and the two highest levels will be discussed in Chapter 10.

Task 7.4   Small group discussion

Look at the following examination questions, and decide which level of learning the student is being asked to demonstrate using the levels of Bloom's taxonomy. Also decide which level of education you think they are suitable for: primary school; secondary school; undergraduate degree; or Masters' degree.

- When was the French Revolution?
- Analyse the social factors which contributed to the French Revolution.
- Contrast the types and uses of public transport in London and Los Angeles.
- Contrast the types and uses of public transport in London and Los Angeles, and suggest possible developments which may improve the air quality in both cities.
- Explain how cheap and rapid international travel can create new health risks, and recommend actions governments should take in response to this.
- Summarize the advantages of eating a balanced diet.
- Describe how a four stroke engine works.
- Compare the uses of telecommunications in the 1960s with the present day.
- Critically evaluate the customer communications strategy of a service company of your choice. Design an alternative strategy and support your recommendations with evidence from research.

Learning tip   Whenever you are preparing any assignment always look carefully at the instructions and notice words like 'analyse', 'apply' and 'evaluate' in the instructions. Teachers often have this taxonomy in mind when they set assignments, and they will not give good marks to students who only repeat ideas taken from textbooks.

Although 'knowledge' and **'comprehension'** are seen in this taxonomy to be the lowest levels of learning, you can also think of them as the foundation of any topic and, so, essential. This is similar to the levels of Marlow's hierarchy of needs you saw in Chapter 1, where it was shown that the lower levels of needs must be satisfied before the higher levels can be achieved.

The movement from 'knowledge' (which is really just repeating things you have found) to 'comprehension' (which is demonstrating your understanding of what you have found) is partly achieved by using your own words to write summaries and paraphrases rather than directly quoting from your sources. This will be looked at in the methods and skills sections below.

Learning tip   Remember this learning tip from Chapter 6: You should make it clear if the notes are your own words or if you have copied an extract from the original. Note down all the details you will need later to include in the reference list, these include: author name and initials; year of publication; title of book, article or journal; publishing details of books (city and name of publisher); volume number and issue number of journals; page numbers.

Approach 2: Making connections

The movement from 'knowledge' (just reproducing information) to 'comprehension' (demonstrating your understanding of a topic) is also achieved by making connections between ideas. You saw when we examined constructivist learning that as you go through a course you should constantly be connecting new ideas to your existing ideas on a topic, and sometimes this means changing your ideas, and perhaps seeing new ways of looking at them.

Learning tip   Look back again to Task 5.3 where we explored the key features of the constructivist learning model. You should get into the habit of reviewing previous readings, exercises, and tasks. Often you can make rapid advances in your understanding by going over ideas again at a later time.

The use of figures – diagrams which help to show the connection of ideas like an image – can help with this. You can use figures in a variety of ways:

- As a method of note-taking, for example when you are listening to a lecture.
- As a method of making more permanent notes, for example summarizing ideas; contrasting different views; showing relationships like cause and effect; or sequences in processes.

- As a way of planning the organization of an assignment you are preparing.
- As visual aids when you are giving oral presentations, which will be explored more in the next chapter.

Task 7.5 Small group exercise

In this book a variety of 'figures' have already been used to help present some quite complex ideas. Work in small groups. First, each of you should quickly draw a sketch of one of the figures previously used to explain these topics (you should try to remember them without looking back):

- Maslow's hierarchy of needs.
- The cultural iceberg.
- Pie charts to show use of time.
- Kolb's learning cycle.

Then can you take it in turns to use your sketches to explain the concept to the other members of your group?

You might find that to explain the figures using words is harder than just using the visual aid of the figure; a picture is worth a thousand words. When you explain a figure you need very exact language to explain the particular connection between ideas.

- '*As a result*': is used to show cause–result connections.
- '*On the other hand*': is used to show connections of contrast.
- '*Subsequently*': is used to show a connection of later time.

These **discourse markers** will be practised in the skills section below.

> **Learning tip** Remember that these figures only represent one way that a situation can be described; different people will understand the situation differently and figure it differently. Such figures can be very useful, but be ready to change, to modify or even to throw away a figure which is no longer useful.

Method 1: Writing summaries and paraphrases

The first method of learning which results from the need to move up to a higher level of learning (to move from 'knowledge' to 'comprehension' in

Bloom's terminology) involves creating summaries or paraphrases, which means that you take ideas from your reading and then rewrite them in your own words. Paraphrases are about the same length as the original text, summaries are shorter. There is still a danger, however, that this will still only create a list of summaries of other people's ideas, and this is still not really making connections. It is much better, then, instead of writing a summary of what one author said on a topic, and then writing a summary of what another author said on the topic and so on, to write one summary of what you understand about a topic based on reading several authors.

Task 7.6   Reading

Read again the student's summary of Maslow's hierarchy of needs in Task 1.3 of Chapter 1. Notice that this is one summary of a topic relying on three sources, rather than three different summaries strung together.

Learning tip   Notice that in this summary the student gives references to the source texts each time an idea is taken, notice also that there are only two direct quotations and these are clearly indicated by the use of quotation marks, but for the rest of the time the student's own words are used. You will find out more about correct methods of referencing in Chapter 11.

These are the steps recommended to produce a summary like this:

- First skim read the original texts, that is to say read them very quickly.
- Then re-read them more slowly and note down the key points.
- Put away the original texts and continue working from the notes you have made.
- Decide if it is possible to connect the points made by different authors.
- Decide if any words or phrases are fixed, for example the way that 'stakeholder' is a fixed term in CSR. You should not try to re-word this, but you may want to consult a glossary to give a definition.
- Decide on the structure you will use to create your summary. This is the key point; this is *your* summary demonstrating what *you* understand as a result of reading, discussing and so on.
- Decide if you want to use any quotations taken directly from the original texts, but not too many, and not too long, as your aim is to demonstrate your understanding by using your own words as much as possible.
- Make a first draft, and check it against the original texts to make sure you have included all the ideas you want.

- Use discourse markers as linking words, ('*thus*'; '*as a result*'; '*whereas*'; '*however*') to show clearly the relationship between ideas.
- Read the paraphrase with an 'editor's eye' checking grammar and spelling.
- Check you have correctly referenced your sources, and have used quotation marks to show the quotations.

The Skills activities below will give practice in this.

Method 2: Lecture note taking

You saw in Chapter 2 that lectures often supply a commentary of the many theories in a module's subject area, and also show how theories are connected, for example how some key thinkers developed the ideas of earlier thinkers, or how one school of thought differs from another. One purpose of the lectures, therefore, is to help students move to a higher level of learning; to move from 'knowledge' to 'comprehension'.

Task 7.7   Pair work

Different people have different methods of taking notes in lectures.

- Some try to copy down everything the teacher is saying, which is really an impossible task particularly if you are studying in a foreign language.
- Some do not really listen at all and instead copy down everything which is written such as PowerPoint slides, which is not a method which will lead to high levels of learning.
- Some use illustrative devices, like arrows to show connections or grids to show contrasts.
- Lots of people use shortened words and phrases; also lots of people use bullet points.

Explain to another student the methods you use, see in which ways you use similar techniques and also if you can learn anything from each other.

Task 7.8   Advice concerning lectures

These are some tips about preparing for and attending lectures, read each point then mark with:

☑☑   = I strongly agree
☑   = I agree
☒   = I disagree
☒☒   = I strongly disagree

It is essential to read about the topic before the lecture, as the lecturer will assume that you have done the course reading so will not explain things you should already know.   □

Arrive on time, as the introduction to the lecture will often explain what is the purpose and structure of the lecture, and how it connects to other topics, so if you miss the introduction you will not understand where the lecturer is going.   □

If the lecturer posts the lecture PowerPoint slides on the VLE there is no point writing down what s/he is saying.   □

Listen in particular for sign-posting phrases which connect the ideas together: '*I will give an example of this . . .*'; '*Moving on to the next obstacle . . .*'; '*This had three important consequences . . .*'.   □

Note down any references the lecturer makes to other things you can read on the topic.   □

Be honest with yourself about things you do not understand, so if the lecturer talks about 'environmental sustainability' and you do not know this term note it down and later look it up.   □

As soon as possible after the lecture re-write the notes, expanding on them and making them more clear so that they will be meaningful months later.   □

If possible, as soon as the lecture finishes discuss your understanding with a class-mate, go to have a coffee together and compare your notes.   □

Remember that your aim is to move your understanding to higher levels, so you are noting what you understand as a result of reading, discussion, and listening to lectures; you should always be trying to connect ideas.   □

Learning tip   One very popular method of taking notes in a way which shows the connection between ideas is known as mind mapping. If you use an Internet search engine and use 'mind map' as a search word you will find many sites which demonstrate this. There is also some computer software which can be used to create complex diagrams such as mind maps. At a simpler level a lot of software has the ability to produce diagrams which can be used as figures to show connection between ideas, for example eco-tourism can be illustrated as a connection between tourism, environmental concern and economic development with a figure like Figure 7.2.

Figure 7.2 Theoretical frameworks for eco-tourism

Skill 1: Glossaries

In Chapter 6 you saw one example of using glossaries to find the meaning of key terms. Every topic has subject specific language, and one part of entering a subject area (of becoming an economist, or becoming a social worker, or becoming a human resource manager) is learning the subject specific language of that topic. It would be a mistake to use a general dictionary to look up these words; instead you should use a subject specific glossary which will give a definition of how this word is used in this subject area. There are now glossaries for every conceivable topic on the Internet, so you should explore several related to your topic area, decide which ones are the most useful for you, then save the links.

Task 7.9   Using glossaries

The theme of this chapter is eco-tourism, so you need to find definitions of subject specific terms related to this topic. Use a search engine to find a glossary of eco-tourism (or a glossary of green tourism), so enter 'glossary eco-tourism' as your search words, then consult several of the sites you find, and look for definitions of these terms:

- Sustainable development.
- Eco-tourism.
- Conservation.
- Environment.

> **Learning tip**   Getting definitions like this is part of learning, of building up your understanding of a topic and, in addition, it allows you to find definitions of terms which can be a useful beginning to a student's assignment. Remember to treat the definitions you use in assignments in exactly the same way that you use any other information from your research: you must decide if you should use your own words or instead use a direct quotation. If you use a direct quotation you must use quotation marks. If you use *either* a quotation *or* your own words you still want to give a reference to show where the ideas come from and to demonstrate that you have read widely on the topic.

Skill 2: Connecting ideas from reading and lectures

At the beginning of this chapter you discussed the links between tourism, development, the environment and corporate social responsibility. A recent development within the tourist industry is known as eco-tourism, or sometimes green tourism, which tries to encourage forms of tourism which balance these different concerns. As with all things you will study at university there are a variety of points of view concerning this topic; there are certain key concepts you will need to define; and there are examples of both good and bad cases which can be used to support different points of view. This topic can be related to the earlier topics you have seen of development and corporate social responsibility. The tasks below, using readings and a lecture, give practice in making connections and changing knowledge to understanding.

Online readings: eco-tourism

On the website connected to this book www.openup.co.uk/international students there is an article concerning eco-tourism:

* Travel Magazine (2002) Eco-tourism: introduction, *TRAVEL AFRICA Magazine*, first published in issue 20. http://www.travelafricamag.com/index2.php?option=com_content&do_pdf=1&id=421

You should then do some autonomous online researching to find the following:

1   A recent international conference concerning ecotourism produced a short document outlining questions and challenges. Use an Internet search engine and look for 'Oslo Statement on Ecotourism' to find a copy of this.
2   You also need some real-world examples to illustrate how principles of eco-tourism can be applied. Use an Internet search engine and the key words 'eco-tourism Africa' or 'eco-tourism India' to find some examples.

3   You need also to read about possible difficulties connected to eco-tourism. Use an Internet search engine and the key words 'eco-tourism problems' to find some articles about difficulties and problems.

Task 7.10   Reading

You should first use the skimming/surveying techniques described in the previous chapter to get a general idea of what these texts include.

Learning tip   Remember the tip from Chapter 6: there is a danger, particularly if you are studying in a foreign language, of trying to read everything intensively and deeply. Use this task to practise the skills of getting broad and general ideas by rapidly reading a large number of texts.

Task 7.11   Listening

On the website connected to this course there is also a short lecture on the topic which links ideas from these readings to some of the other topics you have examined earlier in this course. As you listen to this look at the example of one student's lecture notes which are also on the website.

Task 7.12   Reading

After listening to the lecture you should go back to read the online articles again. This time read them more slowly, and take notes of what you feel are the most important points made in each.

Learning tip   Remember that you should read both before and after any lecture. Lectures are not intended to give a complete understanding of a topic: they aim to support your reading which should always be your main activity. Understanding will not come from your first reading, so re-reading is always necessary.

Skill 3: Discourse markers

Discourse markers are used to connect ideas together, for example to show that one event or situation is a result of another (*as a result*), or follows later in time (*subsequently*), or is an example of something just mentioned (*for example*). In informal situations ideas are often just placed together with no discourse marker and the connection is still obvious: 'I'm hungry. Shall we eat something?' In more carefully thought-out texts, such as in reports and oral presentations of a project, discourse markers are used to make such connections clear.

Task 7.13 Small group work

For each of the following groups of discourse markers one example is given using the topic of tourism and eco-tourism. Make a second example using one of the other discourse markers in each group. Put these in Part B of your portfolio.

* *In addition, furthermore.*
  These are used to show an addition, that the two ideas go easily together.
  Example: *The planned development will create many new jobs and in addition will bring in a lot of money to the local economy.*
  Your example:

* *In the same way, similarly.*
  These are used to show a similarity between two ideas.
  Example: *The local people fear that any changes will destroy the beauty of the area in the same way that other villages along the coast have been damaged.*
  Your example:

* *On the other hand, while, whereas.*
  These are used to show a contrast between the two ideas being connected
  Example: *Most forms of tourism can damage the environment whereas eco-tourism tries to protect and even improve the environment the tourists visit.*
  Your example:

* *However, despite this, nevertheless.*
  These are used to show a concession, that the two ideas may seem to conflict but still exist side by side.
  Example: *The government plans to protect this area, nevertheless permission has been given to build several new hotels there.*
  Your example:

- *Hence, therefore, as a result, consequently.*
  These are used to show that the second idea follows logically from the first.
  Example: *The hotels developments required a lot of water therefore there was less for local people to use for irrigation of their fields.*
  Your example:

- *Subsequently, later, at a later stage.*
  These are used to show a connection of sequence, of the second event coming later.
  Example: *The new facilities will initially include a new road and subsequently a hospital will be built.*
  Your example:

- *Fortunately, unfortunately.*
  These are used to show the writer's attitude to the topic
  Example: *The number of visitors and hence jobs have increased and fortunately this has had little effect on local traditions.*
  Your example:

- *In conclusion, to conclude, to sum up.*
  These are used to show that the next idea is a summary of what has been said.
  Example: *To sum up it seems that the schemes can bring a positive change to the area however it is necessary to keep checking that plans are followed carefully.*
  Your example:

Task 7.14   Portfolio task

This task is to test your ability to take ideas and information from readings in order to write a report. You should try to take ideas and examples from those readings but do not copy out sections, other than short 'quotations' which must be in quotation marks. This involves reading, selecting and writing.

> You have been asked by your local government (for example city or province) to write a report about the possibility of starting an eco-tourism industry locally. The report should be around 1000 words long and divided into sections.

Introduction

Explain what is meant by eco-tourism and how it differs from ordinary tourism. Explain the concept of stakeholders. Explain how this type of tourism has developed. Support this with statistics.

Possible benefits

Explain several of these, and if possible use examples.

Possible problems

Explain several of these, and if possible use examples.

Possible development locally

Refer to one tourist activity already existing in your local area and describe how it can be made more ethical, for all stakeholders and the environment.

Put this in Part B of your portfolio.

Employability link: job advertisements

Look at this extract from a typical job description for a graduate job in human resource management. Notice how many of the job skills required relate to the study skills you have developed already in this book: working autonomously; application of theory to practice; management of time; ability to do a variety of tasks; ability to work in groups; ability to communicate clearly and effectively.

HR MANAGER FOR LARGE RETAIL COMPANY

Knowledge and skills required

- Degree (or equivalent).
- Fully conversant and up to date with all aspects of employment law and HR best practice.
- Experience in the development and implementation of employment policies and procedures.
- Ability to work autonomously and flexibly.
- Influencing, persuading, coaching and negotiating skills.
- Excellent interpersonal, written and verbal communication skills.
- Proactive and self-motivated.
- Excellent planning and organization skills to meet deadlines.
- Cooperative and supportive team player.

Task 7.14   Individual learning plan

Look at other job advertisements, either on the Internet or in good quality newspapers, in particular think about the type of jobs you will apply for after your studies. Notice the skills they are asking for, and start to think about the skills you need to develop during your degree course. Can you make your own **individual learning plan** setting out how and when you intend to develop these skills?

Task 7.15   Critical incident discussion

Critical incidents are descriptions of situations where something has gone wrong, and from them it is possible to glimpse how inappropriate behaviours have resulted from cultural differences. Read through the following critical incident then discuss the questions below. Try to find more than one possible or acceptable answer to each question: the aim is not to find a 'correct' answer, but to see that different explanations are possible for any situation.

A student on a top-up course in marketing got a very bad mark for his first assignment, and the teacher's comment was that the mark was low because he had taken almost all of his ideas from just one book and from the lecture notes that the teacher had posted on the VLE. Another comment was that the student had not followed the assignment instructions carefully. For the second assignment in this module the student first made a plan of the different sections of the assignment, following the instructions exactly. He showed this plan to the tutor who said it was fine. For each part of the assignment the student then found information from a different source, which he carefully copied out into his assignment. In total he has used four books and three shorter articles. He has correctly referenced these.

- What mark do you think the student will get for this second assignment?
- What comments do you think the tutor will make about the second assignment?
- What comments do you think the tutor could have made to the first assignment to help the student do better in the second assignment?
- How will the student feel when he gets the second assignment back?

Reference

Bloom, B. S. ed. (1956) *Taxonomy of Educational Objectives: The Classification of Educational Goals: Handbook I, Cognitive Domain*. New York: Longmans, Green.

8

Group working: what do other people think?

Theme: human resource management – staff training

Aims of this chapter

By the end of this chapter you will have:

- Explored the idea that knowledge is socially constructed.
- Explored the importance of team working.
- Explored the importance of carrying out primary research.
- Become familiar with working in groups to carry out projects.
- Become familiar with the idea of conducting quantitative research.
- Become familiar with the idea of conducting qualitative research.
- Practised designing a questionnaire.
- Practised designing an interview schedule.
- Practised preparing oral presentations.

Introductory exercise: skills training questionnaire

One aspect of Human Resource Management (HRM) concerns staff training, including the following stages:

- Assessing the need for training in different situations of change in an organization.
- Identifying how the training should be carried out.
- Evaluating the effectiveness of it.

The need for constant retraining and upgrading of skills is a feature of modern workforces, and this links to the idea of continuous professional development and keeping a personal development portfolio throughout your career. Reflect on this before completing Task 8.1.

Task 8.1   Examining your own experiences

Complete the following questionnaire about your own skills

IT skills questionnaire

1   Which methods of learning new IT skills have you used?
(*Tick as many as apply*)

    a   Getting friends to show you?   ☐
    b   Having IT training courses at school or college?   ☐
    c   Using online tutorials?   ☐
    d   Just sitting at a computer and trying to do something?   ☐
    e   Training courses organized in jobs you have had?   ☐

2   What are your greatest anxieties related to using IT?
(*use your own words*)

3   Do you consider yourself to be a competent user of IT?

    a   Very competent?   ☐
    b   Competent   ☐
    c   Incompetent   ☐
    d   Very incompetent   ☐

4   What is your greatest need for further IT training?
(*use your own words*)

5   Who do you think should be responsible for supplying this training?

    a   Myself   ☐
    b   My school/college/university   ☐
    c   My employer   ☐
    d   The government   ☐

Task 8.2   Small group discussion

If you are doing this course with a group of other students then compare your IT skills with some classmates, on the other hand if you are following this course alone then discuss your answers to the questionnaire with a friend.

Approach 1: Working in teams

You will find that very often groups of students, usually between three and five, work together on a project over a period of several weeks or even months, and students are often assessed on this type of group work. You have seen that understanding of any situation develops by exploring ideas in groups, so our understanding of a topic is not something we just create on our own, and this was one reason you saw for using discussions in seminars. Doing group project work takes this idea further, as projects often demand extensive work over a period of weeks or even months to investigate some question or problem. After doing this research the group must report their findings sometimes both as an oral presentation and as a written report. This links university education to the world of work, because in your future employment you will often be working as part of a team who need to take advantage of the different strengths and skills of the team members in order to succeed. This requires negotiation, problem solving, coordination and planning. If you are someone who usually likes working alone it is particularly important for you to practise these team working skills. One approach particularly associated with team working comes from the work of Dr Meredith Belbin who believes that people in groups can be divided into different types such as coordinators, team workers, implementers and so on. You can find out more about his ideas at: http://www.belbin.com/

All theories about group working suggest that you should deliberately try to take advantage of the different skills and styles of members, and to work out plans to benefit from the diversity. A team of people can combine their different approaches and achieve a synergy, meaning that the benefits of working together are much more than just adding the skills of the individuals in the team.

Task 8.3   Role play discussion in pairs

Role playing is a method used in some seminar activities. You are going to play the roles of the chief executive officer (CEO) and the director of HRM for a very large car company. You intend to launch a new range of cars onto the market next year. Today the two of you are meeting to decide the skills needed by members for a special project team who will take charge of the launch. These skills will include strategic management, public relations, finance, marketing, market researching, communications and so on. You really want to keep this group small, with no more than five members, so today you will discuss what you believe are the key skills (including personal skills) you want these people to have. Carry out the role play discussion and make notes of what you agree.

Task 8.4   Writing task

After you have decided on the skills the team needs, write an announcement to describe these skills to be sent to all staff in the company in order to attract internal candidates to apply for the project. You can look back to the job advertisement in the Employability link in Chapter 6 for ideas of how to write this. Put this announcement in Part B of your portfolio.

Approach 2: The need for primary research

You have seen that students should be autonomous learners and go beyond the sources of information given to them by their tutors; that is they should set out to find information from a range of different sources. This wide reading is often described as doing research. In this chapter, however, 'research' is used to describe something different; here we are discussing conducting *primary* research. If you think more about the role play in Task 8.3 you can see that at some time the project team who are going to organize the launch of the new range of cars will need to find out a lot of very detailed information about the possible buyers of the cars, that is to say they will need to consult them, to find out how they make their purchasing decisions, and to learn what kind of media (for example newspapers and magazines) they use. They will need to discover what images impress them, and to find out how they will finance their purchase, and so on. Sooner or later they will need to come face to face with intended customers and find out what their likes, preferences, tastes and opinions are. Finding out about these things is one form of primary research, and this is an element of many student assignments and almost all group projects.

Task 8.5   Surveying

As a first step in carrying out primary research you should use the question-naire related to IT training you completed in Task 8.1 and then ask ten other people what are their experiences of these things. Make notes of their responses using the chart below.

IT skills

1   Which methods of learning new IT skills have you used?

1	2	3	4	5	6	7	8	9	10
a	a	a	a	a	a	a	a	a	a
b	b	b	b	b	b	b	b	b	b
c	c	c	c	c	c	c	c	c	c
d	d	d	d	d	d	d	d	d	d
e	e	e	e	e	e	e	e	e	e

2   What are your greatest anxieties related to using IT?

1
2
3
4
5
6
7
8
9
10

3   Do you consider yourself to be a competent user of IT?

1	2	3	4	5	6	7	8	9	10
a	a	a	a	a	a	a	a	a	a
b	b	b	b	b	b	b	b	b	b
c	c	c	c	c	c	c	c	c	c
d	d	d	d	d	d	d	d	d	d

4   What is your greatest need for further IT training?

1
2
3
4
5
6
7
8
9
10

5   Who do you think should be responsible for supplying this
     training?

1	2	3	4	5	6	7	8	9	10
a	a	a	a	a	a	a	a	a	a
b	b	b	b	b	b	b	b	b	b
c	c	c	c	c	c	c	c	c	c
d	d	d	d	d	d	d	d	d	d

Task 8.6   Analysing

Now look at the answers you have collected. Think of a one sentence answer to
each of these questions:

1   What is the most common method of learning a new application?
2   What are people's greatest anxieties related to using IT?
3   What percentages of people consider themselves to be competent
     or very competent users of IT?
4   What are the greatest needs for further training?
5   Who do they think should be responsible for supplying this
     training?

Task 8.7   Writing up

Now join together your answers to write one paragraph.

Congratulations, you have just done some primary research: you used an instrument to collect new information (data); you analysed that information; and then you wrote a brief report concerning your findings. Put this report in Part B of your portfolio.

> **Learning tip**   You will find out more about the need for 'application' of your learning in the next chapter, but for the moment remember that you should be constantly looking outside the university to see examples of the topics you are studying, and asking – the title of this chapter – what do other people think?

Online readings: induction training and research skills

On the website connected to this book www.openup.co.uk/international students there is a reading concerning staff training. Read the article using the extensive reading methods described in Chapter 6, and note briefly what you think are the key points.

1   Accel Team (n.d.) *Planning Employee Training And Development* [online]. Available at: http://accel-team.com/_pdf/05_training.pdf

Then do the following autonomous online researching:

2   Use an Internet search engine and the key words 'induction training' and read at least two different websites, again note briefly what you think are the key points.
3   Use an Internet search engine and the key words 'questionnaire design' and find a checklist for making a good questionnaire.

For the remainder of this chapter you should, if possible, work in a group of around four students to go through the process of group working we are describing. This will involve conducting some primary research then preparing a presentation.

> **Learning tip**   It is likely that you will study a complete module of **research methods** at some time while you are at university, perhaps in connection with writing a final-year dissertation (for undergraduate students), or a Masters' dissertation or thesis. This chapter is just a brief introduction; the intention is to show that doing primary research is exciting – it is not something to be afraid of.

Method 1: Group work

Projects, when used as a form of assessment, often include oral presentations as a part of the assessment; so projects often involve three distinct sets of skills:

- Group working.
- Researching.
- Preparing and giving a presentation.

Think of the topic which the group is researching as a problem which needs to be solved. The group meets first to define the problem, and this is similar to a project in a work situation, for example when a team in a company work together to devise a new product, or to move into a new market, or to change their staff training strategy. The group's task is not to find an answer which already exists, but to create something new by applying their own skills and talents to gather new information, to analyse it and then to come to some form of conclusion such as making recommendations. This can be a challenge as working with other people can be difficult, so you need to develop organizational skills and **interpersonal skills**. Your group needs to agree a method of working, for example how you will resolve disagreements among you, as your individual mark for this module will depend on your group being able to work together even if there are disagreements and arguments.

> **Learning tip** Remember that a discussion in a group is not about winning. Sometimes you may need to accept group decisions which you do not initially agree with in order to keep the cooperation which is necessary to achieve the goal. These are exactly the types of life skills which are needed in work situations, and remember you may pass or fail a module depending on whether you can work effectively in a group.

Task 8.8   Getting to know your group

Spend some time getting to know the other people you will complete this chapter with. Take turns to tell others about your own previous experiences of group working. Think of all areas of your life: sports, clubs or societies, work related situations or previous study experiences.

It is likely that a project will involve a series of meetings where information is exchanged and group decisions are made, and between meetings different group members have their own tasks to do. Remember during the meetings to listen actively to other members of the group, ask questions to get them to add extra information, make sure everyone is included and make sure everyone feels respected.

Learning tip   These days it may be possible to keep in touch with each other between meetings using an online discussion board, and perhaps your course VLE will have this type of facility. If not, you could suggest that your group creates one.

Task 8.9   Preparation for group work

Your task for the remainder of this chapter is to work as a group to research different types of induction training. You have already read something about this, but your group task will require you to carry out primary research – specifically to interview at least four people about their experiences of induction training, and to design a questionnaire which you will ask 20 people to complete. You will then prepare an oral presentation to describe your findings and to make recommendations about best methods for companies to follow. You should now hold your first group meeting to share your individual ideas about these questions.

- How you will resolve difficulties or disagreements?
- Which people can you contact for the interviews?
- Which people can you contact for the questionnaire?
- How can you keep in contact with each other?

Learning tip   If, in any module involving group work, you are asked to keep a portfolio then use it to reflect on any conflicts which arose in the group. Describe what were the causes, how the conflicts were resolved and the role you played. This again is useful and can give you things to talk about in job interviews when employers will be looking for this type of interpersonal skill.

Method 2: What is meant by quantitative research?

Quantitative research involves obtaining information in the form of numbers which you can then use for statistical analysis. This kind of research is often connected to a way of creating knowledge which is called **positivism**. Briefly this approach to knowledge is mostly connected to science, it assumes that by careful and accurate measurement of things in the world, such as weights, volumes, temperatures and so on, it is possible to understand scientific laws – hard facts – and to understand causes and results.

Quantitative surveys (also called questionnaires) are attempts to bring this scientific method into social sciences: a simple example is in market research when consumers are asked to tick boxes about their opinions of a product or a service, and these attitudes can be recorded numerically in what is known as a **Likert scale**, for example:

Very satisfied +2. ☐
Satisfied +1. ☐
Neutral 0. ☐
Dissatisfied −1. ☐
Very dissatisfied −2. ☐

Other ways of making questions quantitative is by giving a list of possible responses and assigning each a number:

The following are the most important factors I consider when choosing a mobile phone (choose up to 3 reasons):
Style. ☐
Cost. ☐
Technical functions. ☐
Size. ☐
Reputation. ☐
Other (supply factor). ☐

The same type of list can be used when you ask the respondents to rank them from 1 (= most important) to 6 (= least important).

One strength of this approach is that you can ask the same questions from a large sample number. Remember, though, that when you choose a sample you must make sure that they really represent the whole group you are researching. For example if you are researching the use of information technology by the staff of a large company you mustn't ask, for example, only young people or just females to fill in your questionnaire as these groups do not represent the whole staff of the company.

Method 3: What is meant by qualitative research?

Qualitative information refers to words. All people, when they try to explain the situation they are in, see themselves in an ongoing story which explains why they are in this situation, what they are doing, if they are succeeding or having difficulties and so on. Importantly, this story is each person's own interpretation of the events they have experienced. Qualitative research is connected to a way of creating knowledge known as **interpretivism**: this is more concerned with each person's view of a situation than with any attempt to understand scientific laws or facts in the outside world. In Chapter 1, Task 1.4, there is a report of some simple qualitative research with international students at a UK university: in one example they were asked 'What is your most important need'? Their answers included:

1 A good group of friends, and a shared hostel room at cheap rates.
2 An electric adaptor as my computer cannot plug in here.

Notice that different people can have very different interpretations of the same situation, the students had different needs. So if, for example, you are studying management and researching the success of a merger between two companies, then you may be able to find some quantitative hard facts (statistics) which everybody could accept (the stock value of the two companies; their market share at any specific time; the number of employees; how many employees lost their job because of the merger). In contrast qualitative information is seen to be softer (but richer and deeper) because all of the people involved, every manager, worker, supplier and customer, will have their own story to tell: for some the merger may be a great achievement, for some a disaster. You saw earlier that one of the aims of quantitative research is the intention to generalize from a sample to a whole population, but with qualitative findings there is no desire to generalize.

There are many ways to collect qualitative data:

- You can get people to write about themselves: research diaries like this can use the kind of reflective writing you have been looking at in portfolios.
- You can organize group meetings, often known as focus groups, where you ask people to talk about a topic: this is used a lot in marketing research, for example when designing packaging for new products.
- You can use interviews.

Task 8.10   Group work

In your group do the two following tasks:

a   Ask all those who feel the temperature in the room you are in is ok to put up their hands, and count the total. Then ask all who feel the temperature in this room is not ok to put up their hands, again count the total.

b   Ask everyone to tell the person sitting next to than how they feel about this room: do they think the chairs are comfortable; is the temperature ok; do they feel relaxed in this room?

Task a produced quantitative information, and it may be possible – for example – to make comparisons between different groups of people. You could, for example, say that most people think that the temperature is okay, but the males were more satisfied than the females.

Task b produced qualitative information, you found out about one person's feelings, and you accept that perhaps each person has a different interpretation of the situation.

Skill 1: Questionnaire design

It is very easy to design a bad questionnaire, so you need to think carefully whenever you make one, and you will always need to pilot a questionnaire with some friends to check that your intentions are made clear.

These are some possible, and very common, design difficulties:

- If the wording is not clear it is possible for different people to interpret items differently, for example *I do not often forget to top up my phone when my credit is low.*
- Some questions may seem intrusive, or the respondents may feel that they are unnecessary, for example questions about age, marriage status or income. Always ask yourself: do I really need this information, and don't ask too many questions.
- Some questions may be biased, that is they may lead the respondent in a certain direction. For example: *I think ThisCola is good because it is refreshing.* Perhaps the people do not think ThisCola is good.
- Some questions may be double-barrelled, so people are unsure how to answer.
  For example: *I often drink tea or coffee for breakfast.*
- Categories, for example when grouping by age:
  15–20; 20–25; 25–30; 30–35. What's wrong here?

Task 8.11 Group discussion

Each method of using a questionnaire brings with it certain problems. Discuss in your project group the problems you might expect with the following ways of delivering your survey, and can you think of how to overcome the difficulties?

- Face to face: stopping people on the street or around the campus.
- Sending the survey by post.
- Sending the survey by email.
- Telephoning people.

Task 8.12   Designing your questionnaire

You will now design your questionnaire about people's experience of induction training they have had when they started new jobs or went to new universities. You want this questionnaire to produce quantitative data. Some of the information you might want to collect would be:

- How many jobs have people had?
- Did they have induction training?
- Was the training useful?
- How long was the training?

You might also want to collect some personal information about the people such as age and qualifications. Decide also which method of delivering the questionnaire you will use.

Skill 2: Interview schedules

Interviews may be structured, unstructured or semi-structured.

- Structured interviews have a list of very specific items, and are very similar to the interviewer just reading out a questionnaire. The advantage of these is that you can compare what different people say on the same topics. The disadvantage is that the questions you ask may not include the topics which these people actually think are the most important.
- Unstructured interviews have no fixed questions, you just ask people to tell you what they think about a topic and then you listen to them and record what they say. Hence it may be difficult to compare what different people say, however it is more likely that people will identify the things they feel are the most important.
- In semi-structured interviews the researcher has a list of topics (called an **interview schedule**), yet lets the interviewees talk about what concerns them, and only when necessary prompts them with a question: 'What do you think about the . . .?'

Learning tip   An important ethical aspect of research is the idea of getting **informed consent** from the participants: this means that you tell them what you are doing and why. For your questionnaire you need to write a sentence to put at the top of your questionnaire to explain the purpose of the research and to promise the participants anonymity. With interviews it is necessary to record the interview, for example by taking notes, or by some form of electronic recording. The idea of informed consent is particularly important if you intend to record people's voices. You must always get their informed consent.

Task 8.13 Designing your interview schedule

You will be using semi-structured interviews of four people for your research about experience of induction training. In your groups you should now agree the interview schedule, remember these are not closed questions but rather prompts to get people talking.

Task 8.14 Carrying out your primary research

You should now use the questionnaire you have designed to get quantitative data from 20 people about their experiences of induction training, and also to use your interview schedule to get qualitative data from four other people. To do this you will need to divide the work between the group members. Remember to follow the principle of informed consent: tell the participants what you are doing and promise them anonymity.

Task 8.15 Analysing your findings

You now need to analyse your findings. Meet as a group and read through the responses you have got.

* What do you think is the most important thing you have found?
* Are there any surprises?
* Can you see any interesting differences between different people's views?
* Did any of the interviewees say anything particularly interesting?

Decide how to present the quantitative data: will you use a grid, or some form of chart? Look again at what the interviewees said, can you select any quotations so that you can use these people's own words to express their opinions? Finally, does your research allow you to make any recommendations about how best to carry out induction training?

Skill 3: Presentations

Group projects are often partly assessed with an oral presentation, and often you will also need to write a report and/or keep a reflective log. Presentations are a method to demonstrate indepth knowledge and they involve an opportunity for face to face questions. Usually an effective presentation involves making a case of some kind: rather than just describing something (a low level of learning) you need to analyse some situation, or recommend actions, or persuade others of the strength of a position.

Task 8.16   Preparation of your presentation

The following stages must be done by the group working together to share the decisions and the tasks.

- Using the ideas you discussed in Task 8.15 you must decide what will be the structure of your presentation, for example: introduction, main points, recommendations and conclusions.
- Then be sure to explain this structure at the beginning of your presentation, so that your audience will be able to follow clearly.
- Then the group must prepare the PowerPoint presentation, and if any members of the group do not know how to do this they should work with someone who does in order to share skills.
- Remember that even if different members of the group prepare some of the slides they should all use the same design and style. It must appear as one professional presentation, not a mixture of individual pieces of work.

Task 8.17   Practising your presentation

Public speaking is a skill which improves with practice, so you must leave plenty of time for preparation and practice. Follow these tips:

- Write brief notes about the key points you are making.
- Do not write a complete script, you are demonstrating your knowledge by being able to talk freely about the topic.
- Each member of the group will need to deal with one part of the presentation, so practise how you will make transitions to hand over to each other.
- Check back to the instructions: have you really done what was asked for?
- Notice the timing, and modify the content if necessary to hit the required timing, for example your presentation may need to be 15 minutes long, and you will lose marks if it is too short or too long.
- As you practise you should make constructive criticisms of each other in order to improve.
- There may be words which you must use which you find difficult to pronounce, so make sure these words are on the slide so your audience can see as well as hear them.
- You may glance at your notes but keep eye contact with the audience, to speak to them, to convince them.
- Make sure that when you refer to a slide (for example if you are explaining a pie chart) you do not turn your back to the audience.
- Do not try to involve your audience by asking them questions, you want to keep control of the presentation.

Task 8.18 Delivering your presentation

You must now give your presentation to an audience, so if you are following this course in a class of students each group must give their presentation to the whole class. The only way to develop confidence is by having more and more practice. After each presentation you must give each other feedback, so go through the points in Task 8.17 above and make comments.

Task 8.19 Portfolio task

This task is particularly important, as you need to look back over what you have done related to the three sets of skills covered in this chapter:

- Group working.
- Researching.
- Preparing and giving a presentation.

Describe what you did, what you felt and what you have learnt about each of these skill sets. Focus in particular on how this experience will allow you to do this type of activity better in future. Put this in Part A of your portfolio.

Employability link

Throughout your time at university, treat every task in the way a professional in the world of work would do that task. The skill of giving presentations is a particular professional requirement: so at all stages of the presentation force yourself to follow professional standards: in the quality of the research; the appearance of your materials; and your own appearance on the day. Make sure that you seize every opportunity in all your assignments to develop your key skills such as working with others, communication, presentation, information technology and problem solving. Remember to keep a record of any examples of this type of activity you do as a student – for example in your personal development portfolio – so that in a job interview you can describe some of the project work you have been involved with, what your role was and what you learnt from it.

Task 8.20 Key skills

It is especially important to keep a record of all training courses you attend, even very short courses such as a half-day session about learning to use a new software program. You should soon have a list of such personal developments which you can describe in job applications and interviews to demonstrate that you are the type of worker who is constantly alert for new opportunities to learn more and to develop. For each of the key skills you first saw in Chapter 5 can you think of a situation where you have developed and demonstrated this skill? Put this chart in Part B of your portfolio.

Skill	Situation
Communication.	
Application of Number.	
Information technology.	
Working with others.	
Improving own learning and performance.	
Problem solving.	

Task 8.21   Critical incident discussion

Critical incidents are descriptions of situations where something has gone wrong, and from them it is possible to glimpse how inappropriate behaviours have resulted from cultural differences. Read through the following critical incident then discuss the questions below. Try to find more than one possible or acceptable answer to each question: the aim is not to find a 'correct' answer, but to see that different explanations are possible for any situation.

> A student was grouped with people he did not know to do a project which involved researching a famous highstreet retailer (different groups were given different retailers to research). They needed to describe their company in detail: its history; its product categories; its current size and market share. They also had to make recommendations concerning the channels of communications the company could develop to be able to communicate better with its customers. The group needed to write up their research as a report and to prepare a poster for a seminar when the different groups would share their findings with the rest of the class. This student found it hard to get along with the other group members, and anyway really prefers to work alone. He therefore did the work alone, and produced a very detailed report and a very effective poster.

- Can you think of some positive aspects of what this student did?
- Can you think of some negative aspects of what this student did?
- In what ways has the student misunderstood the directions he has been given?
- What suggestions do you have to improve the situation?

Part Three

Producing assignments

You saw in Part One of this book that universities are 'cultures of learning' with their own expected ways of behaving. In Part Two you found out about some of the most common methods of studying used in English speaking universities, and saw the sort of things you will be expected to do as a student. You explored *why* you are expected to do these things as well as *how* you should do them. Now the three chapters in Part Three of the book will take you through the stages which you should follow to produce assignments which demonstrate your learning. This involves a change from the *extensive* studying techniques you saw in Part Two (getting broad general ideas) to more *intensive* techniques (going more deeply into specific issues, following the exact requirements demanded in the assignment instructions).

The three chapters in this Part are:

9 What do I have to do to excel in my assessments?
10 What is critical awareness and how can I show it in my work?
11 Finishing off: have I done what was required?

As with Part Two each chapter will explore related approaches, methods and skills.

- **Approaches:** these will outline the theories of learning and teaching associated with this stage of the learning process.
- **Methods:** these will describe the particular behaviours of students and teachers which arise from these approaches.
- **Skills:** these are exercises to develop the study skills (including language and personal skills) necessary for these methods.

9

What do I have to do to excel in my assessments?

Theme: brand management

Aims of this chapter

By the end of this chapter you will have:

- Explored the next two levels of Bloom's taxonomy: application and analysis.
- Explored a process approach to planning assignments.
- Become familiar with analysing assignment titles carefully and precisely.
- Become familiar with establishing research questions.
- Become familiar with using different types of reading texts.
- Become familiar with evaluating the suitability of different sources.
- Practised searching for different types of literature.
- Practised deep reading and note-taking.

Introductory exercise: previous experiences of assessments

Before looking in detail at the process of assessment in English speaking universities it is a good idea to reflect on your own previous experiences, and then to think about how you feel about some of the methods which have been introduced in this book.

Task 9.1   Examining your own experiences

In a small group, first, tell each other about the methods of assessment which you used earlier in your education (for example when you were at secondary school/highschool). What kinds of assessments did you have to do, how many, how often, how long were they? Second, talk about your feelings about the kinds of assignments already mentioned during this course, focusing on presentations, reports, examinations, group work, portfolios.

- Are you excited by them?
- Are you frightened?
- Have you done these sorts of assignment previously?
- Do you feel that these assignments are good methods of assessment?

Online readings: brands

The theme in this chapter concerns the concept of brands, and later you will analyse the instructions for an assignment related to brand management to demonstrate the approaches, methods and skills you will need to do an assignment successfully.

On the website connected to this book www.openup.co.uk/international students there are two readings concerning brands:

1 Jobber, D. and Fahy, J. (2003) *Foundations of Marketing*. London: McGraw Hill Education, pages 128–35.
2 Kerin, R. A., Hartley, S. W., Berkowitz, E. N. and Rudelius, W. (2006). *Marketing*, 8th edn. Boston, MA: McGraw-Hill Irwin, pages 299–302.

You will also need to find some other readings yourself concerning this topic and details of these readings will be given later in this chapter.

Task 9.2   Readings

Read through these two source texts online, and for the moment use the techniques for reading for general information you practised in Chapter 6 in order to get a general understanding. You will look at deeper reading techniques later in this chapter.

Approach 1: Bloom's Taxonomy (application and analysis)

You have already started to examine this important theory concerning different levels of learning, and you saw how to change the lowest level (knowledge) into the next higher level (comprehension) for example by using your own words to report the ideas you have read, and to show the connection between ideas for example by using figures or diagrams. Doing this, though, is only the beginning. Here you will find out how to reach the two next higher levels:

- *Application*: this means that you can use the information you have learned in real world situations, to solve problems.
- *Analysis*: this means that you can break down the information you have learned, to see how the ideas are organized, for example to understand causes of a situation or conclusions which come from it.

To understand why these levels of learning are important you should think again about the definition of an Honours graduate given in Chapter 2, which talked about graduates developing analytical techniques and the skills required to able to make judgements and decisions for solving work related problems. Student assignments are designed so you can demonstrate that you have achieved the intended learning outcomes of your courses, and this chapter will demonstrate how to push your work up to these two next higher levels, to demonstrate analysis and application.

Task 9.3   Pair work

Assignments very often demand that students carry out some form of application of theories they are studying, and this is true for all faculties of a university. Work with another student and try to match the theoretical framework in column 1 with the suitable example of application of theory in column 2. Then you should discuss what you could do to gather the information needed for each of these application activities.

Theoretical Framework	Application of theory
(*Nursing*) Models of patient care.	Investigating how a local bar disposes of empty bottles.
(*Computing*) Theories of human–computer interaction.	Researching experiences of staff in a certain company.
(*Environment*) The waste hierarchy.	Examining a company's mission statement concerning how they check on the conditions of workers in their suppliers.
(*Computing*) Coding theory.	Investigating games console users opinions about the comfort of the design of consoles.

Theoretical Framework	Application of theory
(*Business*) Corporate social responsibility.	Investigating Internet shopping security payments.
(*Marketing*) Brand loyalty.	Surveying tourists about the quality of their hotel accommodation.
(*HRM*) Staff training.	Comparing methods of assessment in universities in different countries.
(*Hospitality management*) Customer satisfaction.	Creating a case study of the care plan for one specific elderly person.
(*e-Commerce*) Internet retailing.	Preparing a questionnaire for customers of a supermarket concerning their shopping.
(*Education*) Cultures of learning.	Interviewing people about their use of online retailers.

Approach 2: Process approach to planning assignments

Your university assignments will never expect you just to repeat what your course has taught you. Your assignments will ask you to do something, for example to solve problems; to make recommendations; to apply theories to practice. Therefore in order to complete any assignment successfully you will need to follow a process such as in Figure 9.1. In this chapter you will examine in detail the first three of these steps, and the remainder of the process will be covered in Chapters 10 and 11.

Figure 9.1   Assessment process

- *Analysing task*: this could take several days of reflection and discussion in order to really understand what is needed.
- *Making a plan*: you need to decide the different sections which the finished assignment could have, and hence to decide which information you need to gather (your research questions).
- *Researching*: this could take two or three weeks for an assignment in the first year of an undergraduate degree, but several months when you are writing a dissertation in your final year or doing a Masters' course. Notice that here *researching* can mean both autonomous reading and carrying out some form of primary research.
- *Making a decision*: you will see in the next chapter that after researching you will need to make a decision about what you think and believe in order to demonstrate critical thinking.
- *Amending the plan*: in the light of the ideas you find during the research, and of your decision concerning the topic, you may need to make changes to your first plan.
- *Writing up*: make sure that your writing follows the structure you have planned; that the ideas are clearly and simply expressed; that you respect the rules of referencing and avoid plagiarism; and that the finished assignment does what the instructions demanded.
- *Editing*: all writers – particularly good writers – spend a lot of time going over a piece of writing to remove errors or to make their ideas more clear, for example putting in phrases to show the connection of ideas like *'for example'*, *'as a result'*, *'in contrast'*. Also pay attention to your IT skills: does your assignment look professional?
- *Submission*: assignments must be handed in on time, perhaps to some specialized assignment handling office.

What do students say?

Student from England:

It is very important to realise that an assignment will take longer than you think. It's a long process and in my case it would usually be about six weeks. I would look at my question, I would carry out my research, I would write my answer and then I would go back and edit what I'd written. You should usually aim to write more than you are actually going to put into your assignment at the end so that you can go back and edit it out.

Student from China:

I strongly agree because I think that doing an assignment is a long term process, and I find that time management is a very important skill which you need for doing assignments. Because you start with the understanding of the questions as a first stage, and then you start to structure your ideas, to do your research, and then you start writing and doing referencing, and then you go back to editing. It takes a very long time to get a good mark.

Method 1: Analysing assignment titles

Look at these example instructions taken from an assignment about branding for students of Marketing:

Assignment brief

The concepts of developing brands and of brand management are well established in commercial areas such as food retailing, fast food restaurants and clothing. Most such companies invest heavily in creating and defending a brand image to differentiate themselves from their competitors. However, more recently there has been a growing understanding that charities (not-for-profit organizations) need also to build and manage their brands in order to compete with other charities for public attention and donations. For this assignment you are going to analyse a charity's current use of branding, then to carry out some primary research to discover how effective its branding strategy is. You will then write a report for the senior managers of that charity to recommend improvements you believe it should make. You need to choose which charity you are going to analyse, and then to notify your tutor of your choice before you start the primary research.

In this assignment you should first explain why concepts such as brand identity and brand image are important, and report on recent published research to explain why these concepts are also important for charities. In addition you need to demonstrate application of your learning: you should choose one example of a charity and analyse the communications it uses, then conduct some primary research using either a quantitative survey or qualitative interviews. In your report you should comment critically on this charity's use of branding. You need also to make recommendations of how this charity can improve its public profile.

For this assignment you should use a report format: a title page; a contents page; an executive summary; theoretical background; the case study; your findings from primary research; your recommendations. (Max 1500 words). You should follow the Harvard referencing system and include a list of references. Any examples of the charity communications should be included as an appendix and are not included in the word count.

Note this is only a simple example; expect the assignments on your degree courses to be far more complex than this.

Task 9.4   Small group work

- First, highlight what you think are the key words in the instructions above.
- Second, make a plan of the structure that you think this report should have.
- Third, decide how many words you would want to use for each part of the report.

Method 2: Creating research questions

When you have decided the structure of your assignment you need to make a list of research questions, meaning a list of the things you need to find out, either by wide reading or by carrying out primary research, or even by doing both. These are some research questions a student prepared for the example assignment above:

- What is meant by branding, brand image and brand identity?
- What is meant by brand management?
- What well-known examples of retailers can I find to illustrate this?
- What are charities (not-for-profit organizations), how many are there, and how important are they in society?
- How do charities raise money?
- What recent research can I find connecting charities to branding?
- Which charity can I find to analyse as a case study?
- Can I find any reports concerning this charity's plans to develop a brand image?
- Can I find any examples of this charity's communications to demonstrate its attempts to build its brand?
- Which primary research methods shall I use?

Task 9.5   Small group work

Look back to the plan of the report you made in Task 9.4. Now decide where in the report you would put your findings for each of the research questions above.

Method 3: What is the literature?

You have seen that in any assignment you need to demonstrate that you understand complex ideas and concepts, and you also need to find up to date examples of these theories in practice. This means you cannot just repeat what you have read in text books but in addition you must use journal articles, news reports, and information from the Internet. For example if you are studying media or communication studies, you may need to find examples of an organization's communications with its clients, for example leaflets produced by a hospital for its patients, and explore how these can be improved; or if you are studying human resource management you may need to discover the methods of staff training a real-world company uses, and evaluate if the methods are suitable.

For many assignments it is possible to think of three types of literature:

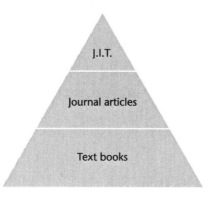

Figure 9.2   The literature pyramid

- Journal articles, these report research findings.
- Text books, these are your sources of established theories and models.
- Just-in-time (JIT), up to date information from news or Internet.

Textbooks

Your module or course guides will identify the text book (or books) most suitable to support your course. You should remember, however, that all introductory books about economics, for example, really cover the same theories. Remember also that every topic has vocabulary and concepts related to it, and these concepts will usually be the topics of weekly lectures and seminars, and your module guide will direct you to each week's reading.

> **Learning tip**   Remember that the concepts you will study are difficult, you will not understand them the first time you look at them. However, by reading various sources and using glossaries to build up your knowledge of the vocabulary of the topic, your understanding will gradually develop.
>
> Explaining these key concepts is often the starting point of an assignment. The best way to prepare for all assignments is:

- Attend all sessions and keep up with the week by week reading.
- Look at a range of textbooks on the topic in your university library.
- Look up the topic of your assignment (for example brand management) in the index (at the back of most text books).
- Note down all the sources you use so that you will be able to reference them correctly later.

Journal articles

These report the findings of research. They usually begin by describing what is already known about a certain topic (often called a 'literature review') and very often this describes the history of a concept and the different schools of thought which have emerged. They will then describe the specific situation that this piece of research has investigated, for example the research might have been to see what are the obstacles to wide spread acceptance of Internet banking in Italy; or to assess the success of a merger between two European car companies; or to see how a certain local government deals with its urban waste. The articles will then describe the research approach and methods they used, for example analysing company documents, or conducting some kinds of primary research. Then they will present their findings and discuss what these findings have added to the discussion described earlier in the literature review. Often they will end with some recommendations. As you progress with your studies expect to use more and more examples of this type of research article.

Learning tip Again your module or course guide may direct you to some journal articles, but you should always try to find appropriate (and hopefully recent) articles yourself. Journal articles these days are increasingly available in electronic format, which you will be able to access from your university library catalogue.

Just-in-time, up to date information

You also want to include the most recent information, for example a company's market share this year, or information about a merger between companies taking place currently, or recent stock market movements. This kind of very recent information is only available on the Internet or in newspapers.

Learning tip You need to be very cautious about which Internet sites and media you can trust. The Skills sections below examines how to evaluate this type of source.

Method 4: Changing research questions into a research plan

A student was given the following title for an essay:

> *'Analyse the advantages for the US resulting from China joining the World Trade Organisation.'*

She analysed the title and created the following research questions:

- What are the reasons for countries trading with each other?
- What is the World Trade Organisation?
- What are the conditions for membership?
- How does membership affect a country's ability to trade?
- What was the level of trade between China and US before China joined the WTO?
- What is the current level of trade between China and the US?
- What benefits does the US get from these changes?

From the research questions she then made a research plan, of where she decided to look for the information:

Research questions	Information to gather: research plan
What are the reasons for countries trading with each other?	Get information about the theory of trade – look in economics text books, also look in journals for recent applications of trade theory to US–China trade (may need to balance contrasting theories).
What is the World Trade Organisation? What are the conditions for membership?	Get information from the Internet: find summary of the WTO – history, aims, objectives, mission statement. Find recent newspaper articles about China meeting the conditions.
What was the level of trade before China joined the WTO? What is the current level of trade between China and the US?	Need to get statistics from official sources (Internet and media), breakdown into value and types of commodities traded.
What benefits does the US get from these changes?	Journal articles and newspapers. Get several views of changes, contrast these.

Task 9.6 Small group work

Take the list of research questions about branding and charities in Methods 2 and decide which type(s) of literature will be the best sources for each question: textbooks, journal articles or newspapers/Internet sites.

Skill 1: Evaluation of Internet websites and media sources

Sources at the bottom and middle of the literature pyramid (books and journal articles) have been **peer reviewed**, that means they have been checked by other academics and you are sure you can use them safely. The higher up the pyramid you go the more carefully you need to take responsibility yourself for assessing the reliability of your sources, and most importantly you need to be careful about Internet and news sources. This requires you to evaluate each source you use, so you must decide yourself:

- Is this source reliable?
- Is it up to date?
- Is it written by someone who can really claim to be an expert?

> **Learning tip** Online journals and e-books are becoming increasingly important. Although these are electronic sources they have been peer reviewed in the same way as printed journals and books, so you can use them safely.

Task 9.7 Pair work

Use an Internet search engine and the search words 'sugar health', then select three different sites and complete the following analysis of them.

What is the appearance of the site? Serious sites are unlikely to have flashing colours or musical soundtracks.		
Site 1:	Site 2:	Site 3:
Is it possible to identify the author, this may be either an individual or a 'corporate author' (for example a company or an organisation).		
Site 1:	Site 2:	Site 3:

Does the site give references to academic sources?		
Site 1:	Site 2:	Site 3:
What does the URL tell you about the website? (for example .ac.uk = a British university, .gov.uk = a government department.)		
Site 1:	Site 2:	Site 3:
What is the main aim of the site? (To entertain, to inform, to sell products or services, to make you share a political or religious idea?) Check the home page.		
Site 1:	Site 2:	Site 3:
When was it last updated? (Remember that often you are using the Internet to find up to date information, so if the site has not been regularly updated it is of no use to you.)		
Site 1:	Site 2:	Site 3:
Does the site have links to other sites which are reputable? (Are the links working?)		
Site 1:	Site 2:	Site 3:
The most important (most critical) question you must ask is 'Can I use this site?'		
Site 1:	Site 2:	Site 3:

Different types of newspapers

In the UK the national daily newspapers can be divided into three groups: quality newspapers (also known as broadsheets); midmarket papers; and redtops (also known as tabloids). As with Internet sites, your decision about what newspapers you can use depends on the purpose of your research. If you are researching popular culture you might want to look at some of the tabloid newspapers, for example to see how different newspapers report current events, but in general it would not be suitable to use tabloids if you are searching for reliable facts. Instead use one of the broadsheet newspapers which has a searchable online archive, for example the *Guardian*.

> **Learning tip**   Imagine that you are doing an assignment about retailing in the UK and you need some just-in-time (very recent) information. If you go to the *Guardian* site http://www.guardian.co.uk/ and use the search terms: 'supermarket AND market share' you will find many very recent and very reliable sources of information.

Skill 2: Deep reading

To prepare for the deep reading exercises you need to find some articles connected to the topic of branding and charities to supplement the two extracts from textbooks you skimmed in Task 9.2.

Task 9.8   Locating research articles

If you are already at a university you should use the university portal for finding research articles. Use the key words 'charity AND brand' to search through the electronic journals your university has subscribed to. (Notice you should use CAPITAL LETTERS for the word AND as this tells the search engine to look for articles containing both 'charity' and 'brand').

> **Learning tip**   If you do not know how to use the university portal then go to your university library helpdesk and ask. Do not be shy of asking for help like this as librarians actually enjoy helping people to find information – it is why they became librarians!

If you are not yet at university use a search engine and the key words 'journal charity brand'.

> **Learning tip**   Some journals will ask you to pay to download articles, but just ignore those articles and keep looking, you will be able to find free ones.

Task 9.9   Locating news articles

You also need some recent news reports about charities and their use of branding. The following are the home pages of four UK broadsheet newspapers which have searchable archives.

* http://www.guardian.co.uk/
* http://www.independent.co.uk/
* http://www.telegraph.co.uk/
* http://www.timesonline.co.uk/tol/news/

Use the key words 'branding AND charity', and if possible set the search facility to search by 'relevance' rather than 'date' (if you do not it will first find the most recent articles about either charities or branding rather than finding the articles which are about both branding and charities).

Task 9.10   Choosing your example charity

Almost all charities will have a website, so now choose a charity to analyse as a case study, for example in the news items you have found there will certainly be examples given, so find the home pages of these charities and look for examples of their use of branding.

You have already looked at the extensive techniques of skim reading and scan reading, you will now find out about intensive reading, which is more directed to get deeper information, for example when researching for an assignment. Think of extensive reading as being wide and intensive reading as being deep. Reading is a spiral process: you should go over each text several times, and you should never begin by deep reading. Follow these steps with the articles you have just located.

Step one. Decision: is this text going to be useful?

If an article begins with an abstract then you should read this to help decide if it is going to really be useful. Articles which you have found using key words in search engines or data bases may be in fact be about something very different from the topic you need, so you do not want to waste time on them.

Step two. Skim read: what is the structure of this text?

After you decide that an article (or chapter) may be worth reading you should first skim through it to get a general idea of what it is about. During this skimming make use of anything like section headings or diagrams to help get an idea of the structure of it.

Step three. Decide which sections you need to read deeply

Perhaps some parts of the article are more useful for you than others, and there may be some sections which you will not need to read deeply, on the other hand perhaps there are some sections which will be very useful. Even if a text does not have section headings it will be arranged in paragraphs, and the introduction should give a clear idea of the structure. Remember the surveying technique described in Chapter 6, each paragraph should begin with a key topic sentence, so often it is a good idea first to read only the first sentence of each paragraph.

Step four. First reading: note the connection of ideas

If you decide that the article is relevant (or at least a part of it is relevant) then start to read it more slowly and carefully, but do not panic if at first you do not understand it – this is a part of learning. Highlight any discourse markers to help see how the parts of the text are connected, for example:

- *For example*
- *As a result*
- *The second objection*
- *On the other hand*
- *First . . . Second . . . Third . . .*

Step five. If necessary look up specific terms elsewhere

Remember you saw in Chapter 7 that every field or domain (for example HRM, or finance, or media) has subject specific vocabulary; so you should use glossaries to look up subject specific vocabulary. Remember that part of studying a subject, particularly for new students and students whose first language is not English, is learning this subject specific language.

Step six. Second reading: make notes which you can use later

In order to use this text in your assignments you will need to record all the information necessary to reference it accurately (you will find out more about referencing in Chapter 11).

Step seven. Read other texts in the same way

The concepts you are studying are difficult. It is not likely that you will get a clear and detailed understanding of a topic by reading just one article. Different writers will explain things differently, they will illustrate with different examples, indeed they may have different points of view.

Step eight. Come back and re-read the earlier texts

People often describe two different types of understanding; it can be like suddenly turning on a light bulb, but much more often it is like making a large snowball by first rolling a small snowball down a hill. You should expect understanding to come gradually as you read more and more, just like making the snowball.

Task 9.11   Portfolio task

You should now have a selection of reading texts on the topic of branding, and branding concerning charities. These different texts should represent the pyramid of texts described earlier; they include extracts from textbooks, research articles, and recent just-in-time news reports and Internet sites. Now look back to the research questions listed in Methods 2 about the example assignment: can you find information about these questions in the articles you have found? Do not try to write the complete report; just make notes based on your reading for each of the questions listed. You may find that you need to do some more research to get information about every research question. Put your notes in Part B of your portfolio.

Employability link

The report writing assignment described in this chapter is a good example of how learning outcomes should be connected to professional standards. Notice that the specifications about length and structure are very precise; above all the report has a specific purpose (to make recommendations) and a specific audience (the senior managers of a charity). A report in a business setting must be 100 percent perfect: there can be no errors in language such as grammar or spelling mistakes. You also need high level IT skills to produce a report which is clearly presented and easy to read.

Task 9.12   Critical incident discussion

Critical incidents are descriptions of situations where something has gone wrong, and from them it is possible to glimpse how inappropriate behaviours have resulted from cultural differences. Read through the following critical incident then discuss the questions below.

Try to find more than one possible or acceptable answer to each question: the aim is not to find a 'correct' answer, but to see that different explanations are possible for any situation.

> A student of nursing had an assignment which included comparing different models of nursing care for elderly people. One part of the assignment required her to carry out some primary research by interviewing one patient in the hospital where she did her nursing practice placement and then to recommend a care plan for that patient. As the student was rather shy and embarrassed about her level of English she decided not to do this primary research and instead used a case study taken from one of the textbooks used on her course.

- Can you think of some positive aspects of what this student did?
- Can you think of some negative aspects of what this student did?
- In what ways has the student misunderstood the directions she has been given?
- What suggestions do you have to improve the situation?

10

What is critical awareness and how can I show it in my work?

Theme: reviewing the themes of motivation, CSR and brand management

---

Aims of this chapter

By the end of this chapter you will have:

- Explored the two highest levels of Bloom's taxonomy: synthesis and evaluation.
- Explored what is meant by critical awareness.
- Become familiar with ways of developing critical awareness when you are reading and note-taking.
- Become familiar with ways of devising a plan and a structure for your writing.
- Become familiar with ways of demonstrating critical awareness in your writing.
- Practised synthesizing information and building paragraphs.
- Practised incorporating qualitative research into your assignments.
- Practised incorporating quantitative research into your assignments.

Introductory exercise: the difference between description and evaluation

Examine your own experiences with another student: tell each other about your favourite snack, using two distinct stages:

- First, describe the snack as in a factual report. Try to do this as scientifically as possible without talking about your feelings in any way; explain what the snack is made of, how it is prepared, where this snack originated.
- Second, be very personal. Try to explain when you first discovered it, why you like it, when you usually eat it, and how you feel when you eat it.

The first part of your discussion is *descriptive* as you are just talking about the snack; the second part is *evaluative* as you are talking about how you feel about it.

In the previous chapter you started to examine the first stages of preparing an assignment connected to charities and branding. You saw that a common reason for a student failing an assignment is not analysing the task appropriately, so not producing what has been asked for. In this chapter you will look at the next steps in the process, and you will see that in order to get high marks for an assignment (that is to say more than just passing) it is necessary to move from being descriptive (meaning just reporting what you have found) to being evaluative or critical.

Approach 1: Bloom's taxonomy (synthesis and evaluation)

You have already looked at the first four levels of this theory of learning, and found that by following the instructions for an assignment carefully you can push yourself to higher and higher levels. Here you will see how to reach the two highest levels:

- *Synthesis*: this means that you can combine and connect the ideas and information you have learned and use them in new contexts. Synthesis has the idea of connecting ideas and building up something new and original.
- *Evaluation*: this means that you can make a decision concerning how you value the end-product of the information you have learned, for example you can compare different models or theories and decide which is best for a certain situation.

You have seen that each course or module has clear intended learning outcomes (ILOs) and that by following the detailed instructions for assignments you can demonstrate that you have achieved these outcomes. Your university will also have **assessment criteria** (see Figure 10.1) to explain the **grades** which students are given for their assessments, and these criteria connect the assignment instructions to the intended learning outcomes and to these different levels of learning.

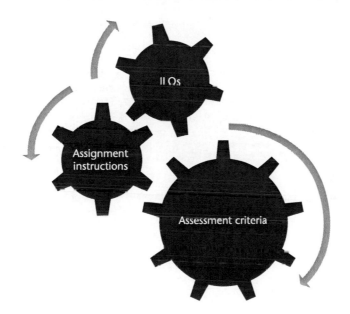

Figure 10.1 Assessment criteria, outcomes and instructions

Task 10.1   Reading

Here is a simple example of what assessment criteria are like (again expect the actual assessment criteria your university uses to be more complex than this): as you read highlight any words which refer to the different levels of learning in Bloom's taxonomy.

Distinction	A	Work of distinguished quality which is based on a rigorous and broad knowledge of facts and concepts of the topic. The work will demonstrate sustained ability to analyse, synthesize, evaluate and interpret concepts, principles and data. Outputs will be communicated effectively, accurately and reliably. The work will demonstrate development of sound arguments and judgements. There will be strong evidence of competence to plan, develop and evaluate problem solving strategies, and of the capability to work autonomously and to self-evaluate.
Strong merit	B	Work of commendable quality based on strong knowledge of facts and concepts of the topic. There will be clear evidence of analysis, synthesis, evaluation and application. The work will be very well organized and communicated, and will demonstrate good use of skills relevant to the task. There will be consistent evidence of capability in all relevant key skills, including the ability to self-evaluate and work autonomously.

Merit	C	Work of sound quality based on a firm knowledge of facts and concepts of the topic. The work will be mostly accurate and provide some evidence of the ability to analyse, synthesize and evaluate, and it will be well organized and communicated effectively. There will be good evidence of ability to take responsibility for own learning, and to demonstrate competence in relevant key skills.
Pass	D	Work of generally satisfactory quality covering the facts and concepts of the topic. The work will be largely descriptive with little evidence of analysis, synthesis, evaluation or application. There may be some misunderstanding of key concepts/principles. The work will be appropriately presented and organized. There will be some evidence of ability to operate with autonomy, and to demonstrate relevant key skills.
Fail	F	Work that falls well short in relation to one or more area of knowledge or key skills. It may address the assessment task to some extent, but such satisfactory characteristics will be clearly outweighed by major deficiencies across remaining areas.

Task 10.2   Pair work

During this course you have looked at several aspects of the culture of learning in English speaking universities, including the need to be autonomous learners, to be reflective, to present work at a professional standard, to use knowledge to solve problems or make recommendations and to demonstrate the higher levels of learning (application, analysis, synthesis, evaluation). Work with another student and complete the following table by taking phrases from the example assessment criteria above to show the difference between work which would just be a pass and that which would be a distinction.

	Pass (D)	Distinction (A)
Autonomous learning		
Reflective learning		
Presentation of work		
Development of key skills		
Problem solving/making recommendations		
Levels of learning		

Task 10.3   Pair work

Now look back to the example assignment brief in Chapter 9 and compare it with the assessment criteria above: together make a list of the things you think it would be necessary to do in that assignment in order to get a distinction.

Approach 2: Critical awareness

You will find that most assignment instructions state that students should demonstrate 'critical writing', 'critical thinking', or 'critical evaluation', and university teachers frequently tell students that their marks are low because they have not done this. For example the assignment instructions you saw in Chapter 9 included this: 'In your report you should comment critically on this charity's use of branding'.

Learning tip   A very common misunderstanding – and a dangerous misunderstanding – is to think that in an assignment a student should try to give a balanced review of a topic (balancing different opinions, or balancing positive and negative aspects of it), and that the student should then only express their opinion on the topic in a short final concluding paragraph. This type of writing is often taught on academic writing courses, for example if students are preparing for an IELTS examination, but this type of essay does not bring you to demonstrate the levels of learning which universities really respect. This misunderstanding is dangerous because it leads to writing which is just description or reproduction, and if you look at the assessment criteria above you will see that this can only get a grade D.

Task 10.4   Small group discussion

Being 'critical' is a difficult concept to understand, it may be a completely new way of learning for some students, and it can be a difficult skill to develop. If you look up the word 'critical' in a dictionary you will find it has many uses, and the following list of definitions is adapted from just one online source:

1   A tendency to find and call attention to errors and flaws: 'a critical attitude'.
2   At or of a point at which a property or phenomenon suffers an abrupt change: 'a critical temperature of water is 100 degrees C'.
3   Characterized by careful evaluation and judgment.
4   Urgently needed; absolutely necessary: 'critical medical supplies'.
5   Forming or having the nature of a turning point or crisis: 'a critical point in the campaign'.

6   Being in or verging on a state of crisis or emergency 'a critical illness'.

7   Involving or characteristic of critics or criticism 'critical acclaim'.

(Adapted from WordNet:
http://wordnet.princeton.edu/perl/webwn?s=critical)

Discuss with some other students which of these definitions is the one you think is intended in student assignment instructions. (**Tip:** the answer is the definition which is linked closely to the two highest levels of Bloom's taxonomy.)

What do teachers say?

Lecturer in information systems:

Being critical involves seeing a topic in comparison to other answers and frameworks, and also seeing it related to specific environments to question appropriateness.

Advisor in centre for academic practice:

It's the ability to stand back from an opinion, issue, or set of ideas and ask pertinent questions in order to synthesize and see different perspectives.

A report from Higher Education researchers:

the willingness to question material encountered, to form opinions and be assertive about expressing viewpoints, in other words, to be aware of the contestability of knowledge.

(Caruana and Spurling 2007: 56)

Method 1: Developing critical awareness when you are reading and note-taking

Remember the two different types of understanding described in the previous chapter: one which is like suddenly turning on a light bulb, and one which is like making a large snowball by first rolling a small snowball down a hill. Critical thinking is usually like the snowball, it comes from a process of seeing that there are different viewpoints concerning any topic, and noticing that people produce evidence of varying quality to support their viewpoint, it comes from discussion and reflection; it comes from re-reading texts more than once.

> **Learning tip**   Critical thinking develops over time; pay careful attention to the feedback you get from teachers about each of your assignments, and follow the advice they have given when you produce your next assignments.

You have looked at two types of reading already; in Chapter 6 you looked at extensive reading and taking notes to make summaries or paraphrases about a text, and in Chapter 9 you looked at intensive reading and making notes about particular specific information you have decided you need to include in an assignment. Here you will look at a third type of reading and note taking, reading for critical awareness, which involves asking questions both about the text and about your feelings about the text.

In order to be critical when you read a text you need to question all the claims made in it, so instead of just making notes about what an author says about the topic you should try to make notes about what you think about a topic as a result of reading what an author says. If you think the text is making a good point note down both what the point is *and* that you think it is a good point. If you think it is stronger or weaker than the argument of another author then note this down too. In this way you are beginning to develop your critical opinion rather than just reproducing other people's ideas.

Task 10.5   Online reading

You should practise your autonomous studying skills to find some more online readings on one of the three topics you have used already in this course: motivation, CSR and brand management.

> **Learning tip**   Use an Internet search engine and think carefully about the key words you use. Remember you can use 'AND' to find sites which concern specific topics: 'motivation AND workers'; similarly you can use 'NOT' to exclude certain topics: 'Brand Management NOT fashion'.

As you first look at each site go through the steps of evaluating its suitability by following the procedure you saw in Chapter 9, Task 9.7. If you decide the article is suitable then first read it very quickly before re-reading it more critically, ask:

- Is this article based on research?
- Was the research good quality?
- Are there alternative theories?
- Has this been applied in practice?
- Add other questions: get into the habit of interrogating a text rather than just accepting everything it says.

Method 2: Devising a plan and a structure for your writing

At the end of Chapter 9 you reviewed concepts related to branding and charities, and you made some notes based on reading different types of articles. A report just based on those notes would only be descriptive, that is it would only be describing what other people had said. However, your writing can only be critical when you decide your own position about a topic and then write an assignment which clearly shows (at all stages of the structure, and not just in the short conclusion) what your position is and how it results from reading, questioning, and evaluating existing literature and research findings.

The next key step in Figure 9.1 which you saw in the last chapter is 'making a decision' and you must do this before you can make your final plan for producing the assignment which will demonstrate your critical thinking. Making this decision is therefore a crucial step; before you start writing you need to make a plan, and before you can make the plan you need to have decided what your position is (this is really the reason for the research you do for each assignment).

When you are preparing an assignment this decision is a result of all the earlier stages in the learning process:

• The extensive reading when you started the course.
• The learning of the subject specific concepts/language.
• The lectures you attended and the seminar discussions you have had.
• The intensive research which resulted from analysing the assignment instructions.
• The practical examples you investigated.

This decision then informs all of the later stages in the process of producing the assignment and will give the text you are writing a structure and a destination: a clear explanation of your position.

> **Learning tip** The assignment instructions should explain what sort of destination this will be: recommendations, decisions, evaluations, etc.
> In order to explain your position on the topic, and to explain why you think the way you do, you need to evaluate the evidence and arguments of the sources you have read. Your position is justified in every step of the assignment, not just in the conclusion.

Task 10.6   Group discussions

The discussion questions below are related to four topics you have explored earlier in this book. Take the topics in turn and discuss each one in a group.

You are not trying to come to an agreement, but it is necessary for each student to articulate clearly what is their position concerning each question.

- Concerning development: do you think that economic growth is essential before social improvements can happen?
- Concerning Maslow's hierarchy of needs: do you think companies should try to satisfy their workers lower level needs if they want them to work well?
- Concerning eco-tourism: do you feel it is possible to develop a tourist industry which does not damage the environment?
- Concerning HRM: what do you think are the best methods for improving the IT skills of staff?

Task 10.7 Writing

Here are three examples of what different students decided about a question concerning development:

> 'In the world now there are developed and developing countries. Sometime in the future all countries will be developed'. Do you agree with this statement?

You should notice that none of these are trying to guess what the teacher may think is the 'correct' answer; they are clear statements that show these students have each studied the topic and have come to a clear decision about what they think. Each of these students will now be in a position to write an assignment which demonstrates their critical thinking.

Student 1

I think that development is really about economic growth, because that is what people want, and all other things – such as building hospitals – need money. I think that there is no limit to the amount of growth which is possible because we will always find new resources and technology. There will probably always be some people richer than others, but in the future everybody can be much more developed than now.

Student 2

I think that economic growth is the cause of the poverty of many people in the world, it consumes energy and creates pollution, it needs a large number of poor people to work for low wages, so these people will never have social development in the current world order. The only way all people will become developed is if we have a complete change in the way the world is run, if we move away from the ideas of economic growth and replace them with the ideas of sustainability and basic needs.

Student 3

I think that development is really about economic growth, and that is what most people want, but I think that there are not enough resources for everybody to get rich. I think the rich are powerful, so they will prevent the poor countries getting power. So I think the gap between developed and developing will always be there.

Now for each of the four questions you discussed in Task 10.6 write a short paragraph to explain your opinion on the topic. Begin with the words 'In my opinion . . .'.

Learning tip   Note, you will not actually include this paragraph in a written assignment, but this first step of taking time to clearly outline what you think on the topic will allow you to then make a plan of an assignment. Your work will then demonstrate that you have thought critically and have come to a decision, so your assignment will not just repeat what you have read but will present your opinion informed by what you have read.

Method 3: Demonstrating critical awareness in your writing

Before you start writing, after completing your research and deciding where you stand on the topic, you should amend the assignment plan you made earlier; the plan you devise now should be a list a series of steps which will take the reader on a journey which will explain why you came to believe what you do believe.

The following suggestions will help you to demonstrate critical awareness in your writing.

- Make sure that you do plan your writing. If you are not clear in your own mind what the structure of your writing is then your readers will certainly not have a clear idea either. Planning your writing is therefore essential.
- A report (for example the one described in the example assignment on branding and charities in Chapter 9) will have section headings which help

to give the whole report a clear structure. An essay, on the other hand, does not have section headings. It is a good idea, however, temporarily to use headings during the early stages of writing an essay; this will ensure that each part has a clearly defined purpose.

- Similarly, although the finished essay will be written in impersonal style (without direct reference to yourself), in the early stages deliberately refer to yourself, your position and your intentions. (Say: *'In my opinion . . .'*, *'I believe . . .'*).
- Later you will need to edit out the section headings (and replace them with topic sentences which you will practise in the Skills section below) and also change the personal style of writing to an impersonal style.
- Doing these things will ensure that the essay has a clear structure and, most importantly, is built around your position rather than just reproducing the ideas of others.

Learning tip   The process we are describing can take several weeks, and during this time it is easy to go off target, so keep referring back to the assignment instructions to check you are on target.

Skill 1: Synthesizing information and building paragraphs

A text should be a clear progression of ideas made up of a series paragraphs, and the paragraphs should link with each other to create the structure of the argument you are making. Paragraphing is a way of dividing up something complex, the whole text, into smaller units in order to help the reader.

A paragraph explains an idea, it may be only one sentence or several sentences. For example if you are describing a process (for example how a training course should be organized) you may decide to break this down into a series of steps and give each step a paragraph. If you are writing about corporate social responsibility (an example from earlier in this book) you might decide to give each 'view' of this topic (positive, negative, alternative) a different paragraph.

The key word in the above description is *'decide'*: good paragraphing (which really amounts to giving your readers good assistance in following your thinking) is not an accident that just happens, it comes from making clear decisions about the structure of your thinking. Each paragraph should have a clear purpose, and the purpose should be clear from the first (topic) sentence. For example if the paragraph is going to introduce a difficulty it could begin with: 'A difficulty with this approach is . . .'; if the paragraph is going to introduce an example it could begin with: 'Turning to an example of this . . .'. The continuation of the paragraph is some kind of expansion of that idea, it may give further examples, it may give extra details, it may indicate the writer's opinion of the topic, and it may quote other writer's opinions.

> **Learning tip**   When you looked at reading strategies you saw that it is often a good idea to survey a text by first only reading the first sentence in each paragraph. This technique helps us to understand the general structure of a text because the first sentence in a paragraph is usually the topic sentence, so it tells you what this paragraph is about.

Each paragraph should if possible combine ideas from different sources, as this is a simple way of demonstrating your wide reading and also is an example of synthesis. If the purpose of the paragraph is to introduce the idea of economic growth then it could give a definition of economic growth from one source, an example of economic growth from another, and statistics concerning economic growth from a third.

> **Learning tip**   Sometimes you may find that a paragraph has become too long, in which case you will need to divide it up. Then you will need to introduce each of these paragraphs with its own topic sentence.

Task 10.8   Writing topic sentences

These are some of the research questions we found for the assignment brief you saw in Chapter 9. For each one write a suitable first (topic) sentence to introduce a paragraph on that topic. Do not try to write beautiful literary English, be as clear and simple as possible.

- What is meant by branding, brand image and brand identity?
  Topic sentence:
- What is meant by brand management?
  Topic sentence:
- What well-known examples of retailers can I find to illustrate this?
  Topic sentence:
- What are charities (not-for-profit organizations), how many are there, and how important are they in society?
  Topic sentence:
- How do charities raise money?
  Topic sentence:

Skill 2: How to deal with qualitative data

To get a high mark it may also be necessary to incorporate examples of primary research. You saw some basic ways of collecting primary data in Chapter 8, and here you will see how to include your findings in your assignments.

> **Learning tip** Always check the assignment brief carefully to see if it requires you to do primary research, and if you are unsure contact your tutor to see if this is expected.

The purpose of qualitative research is not to try to get generalizable data, and this is one of the differences between this kind of research and the quantitative approach which is based on statistics. Remember that you use fewer participants in this type of research than with quantitative research, but the information you get from each one will be richer and deeper. All people, when they try to explain the situation they are in, see themselves in a story which explains *why* they are in this situation; *why* they are doing this activity; if they are succeeding or having difficulties; and so on. Importantly, this story is each person's own interpretation of the events they have experienced. The aim of the qualitative research is to try to see the world through the eyes of your participants, therefore it is important to take detailed notes in your interviews, or to record what people are saying. You should finish your field research with quite detailed notes which summarize what the people you interviewed (or who took part in focus groups you organized) feel and think. You need to then do two further steps:

- You need to analyse the data.
- You need to present the data.

As you look at your notes you begin to notice that you can 'code' the information. 'Coding' involves reading your notes over several times and noticing certain themes. Here is an example of this procedure. A student carried out some primary research concerning fair trade, which is a topic connected to corporate social responsibility. She wanted to find out if people had heard about fairtrade products, which are often made from the produce of poor countries but which have been marketed in a way to protect the interests of the farmers and communities there. She also wanted to find out if people would be willing to pay more for products like chocolate if that meant better conditions for communities in poor countries. When she read through what different people had said she noticed that some of the comments referred to 'quality', some referred to 'price', some referred to 'ethics' and some to the 'environment'. These then became her codes. One part of her report was:

> Concerning quality there were a variety of views. Some respondents said that they do not buy fairtrade products as they think the main brands represent highest quality: 'I always buy Cadbury's chocolate as I only want to give the best to my children', but others reported a surprise that the quality of fairtrade products is high: 'I really enjoyed it, and yes I will buy it again in the future'.

Notice that you want to include the words that the respondents used as you are trying to report the world as seen through their eyes.

Task 10.9 Primary research practice

In the assignment brief in Chapter 9 part of the instructions were: 'For this assignment you are going to analyse a charity's current use of branding, then carry out some primary research to discover how effective its branding strategy is'. You are not going to do this complete assignment, but for this task you should choose one charity (for example Oxfam which you looked at in Chapter 5) and interview a few people to simply ask:

- Have they heard of this charity?
- Do they know what this charity does?
- Have they ever given money to this charity? (If yes – why? If no – why?)

Then write one paragraph where you group your findings by a theme and include examples of what people actually said. Put this in Part B of your portfolio.

Skill 3: How to deal with quantitative data

Statistics can be descriptive, meaning that they just give a summary of your findings, for example: how many, or what was the mean? Alternatively statistics can be analytic, meaning that you use them to explain correlations between different variables, or differences between groups. For a student of education doing some primary research about examination success of a group of student both of these could be used:

- To present the exam results of a group of children in tables and graphs, and to give the mean of the marks, or the mean ages of the children, s/he would use descriptive statistics.
- To examine the results more deeply, to find if there is a difference between the boys and girls, or between the children of two social classes, would be to use inferential statistics.

> **Learning tip** For this course we are only looking at descriptive uses, but note that analytical statistics are seen as 'higher' levels of researching and you may need to find out more about these later.

Task 10.10 Small Group work

When you want to present quantitative data the three most common types of charts are bar graphs, pie charts and line graphs. Which would be most suitable to demonstrate:

* Changes in numbers of people buying fairtrade goods over the last ten years?
* The occupations of customers in a supermarket?
* The percentages of different types of goods sold in one supermarket (for example fruit, coffee, wine) which are fairtrade?

In your groups make sketches to demonstrate how you would be able to present findings on these topics.

Employability link: employability and globalization

Recent research into employability in a globalized world (Archer and Davidson 2008) shows that employers want graduates who have a global perspective, for example who possess foreign language skills and experience of other cultures. The research found that the top two skills they looked for were communication and team working, which have been main topics of this book. The key skills you have looked at so far can all be given an international aspect: for example communication skills in cross-cultural situations, team working with members from other cultures and so on. Some of these requirements seem to suggest that international students who have studied in English speaking universities should have an advantage in that they will have experienced at least two cultures and may have fluency in at least two languages. You need to do two things, though, to develop this cross-cultural advantage fully: first, you should give exactly the same care and attention to demonstrating your experiences in both situations; second, you should reflect on the differences you have experienced. For example have you found that work teams are organized differently in the two situations? Have you found that decision making processes similar or different? Have you found that channels of communication inside organizations or between organizations and clients are the same or different?

Task 10.11 Crossing cultures

During this course you have discussed a series of critical incidents. Now, using your own knowledge of operating in two different cultures, can you create a critical incident for discussion among your classmates. Try to base this on something you experienced or witnessed which involved some kind of cultural clash. Remember these are descriptions of situations where something has gone wrong, and from them it is possible to glimpse how inappropriate behaviours have resulted from cultural differences. Describe the situation and then list four questions for the class to discuss.

Task 10.12   Critical incident discussion

Critical incidents are descriptions of situations where something has gone wrong, and from them it is possible to glimpse how inappropriate behaviours have resulted from cultural differences. Read through the following critical incident then discuss the questions below. Try to find more than one possible or acceptable answer to each question: the aim is not to find a 'correct' answer, but to see that different explanations are possible for any situation.

A student on a media studies course was told to do some primary research concerning the way different people in the UK follow the news. She designed an interview schedule listing different forms of following the news (including different types of newspapers, different TV and radio stations, online sources, news-to-mobile). She found a questionnaire online about a similar topic which she was able to adapt to get some quantitative data (and she clearly acknowledged where she had taken the questionnaire from and the changes she had made). When the time came to gather the data she was already very busy with several other assignments, so instead of going into the town centre to interview people she decided just to collect data from students on the campus, and because she lived with a lot of other international students most of the responses came from these. She interviewed eight people and got 75 responses to her questionnaire, which was a larger number than her tutor had said was necessary. When she began to write her report she felt very confident that she had done good quality primary research.

- Can you think of some positive aspects of what this student did?
- Can you think of some negative aspects of what this student did?
- In what ways has the student misunderstood the directions she has been given?
- What suggestions do you have to improve the situation?

References

Archer, W. and Davison, J. (2008) *Graduate Employability: The Views of Employers.* London: Council for Industry and Higher Education.

Caruna, V. and Spurling, N. (2007) *The Internationalisation of UK Higher Education.* London: HEA.

11

Finishing off: have I done what was required?

Theme: strategic management

Aims of this chapter

By the end of this chapter you will have:

- Explored the concept of discourse communities.
- Become familiar with methods to avoid plagiarism.
- Practised referencing/citation skills.
- Practised editing skills.

Introductory exercise: review of methods and skills

The table below lists several of the study methods and skills which you have seen earlier in this book. For each one you should carry out a self-evaluation; are you confident that you understand both *why* these behaviours are respected in English speaking universities and also are you sure *how* to demonstrate them in your own study? If you feel there are any aspects you do not feel completely confident with then you should review those sections now. Put your completed evaluation in Part A of your portfolio.

Task 11.1   Self evaluation

☑☑☑ = I understand this well and I am confident I can do this

☑☑ = I have a good idea and I am confident I will become better at doing this

☑ = I am not really sure about this, I need to review this topic

Method/skill	
Use of seminar discussions: I can express my opinions clearly in discussions.	
Reflective Learning: I can think about my progress as I go through a course, and write subjectively about changes, for example in portfolios.	
Extensive reading: I can use quick reading techniques such as skimming, surveying, scanning.	
Autonomous learning: I can find things out for myself.	
Time management: I can plan my use of time for study and social activities.	
Taking notes from readings: I can make summaries of readings in my own words.	
Lectures: I can take notes from lectures.	
IT: I can produce professional quality assignments; word processing, PowerPoint and graphs.	
Group work: I have good group working skills, such as communication, division of responsibilities, planning.	
Presentation skills: I can speak clearly and confidently to a group of people; I can persuade them.	
Critical skills: I can analyse assignments to create research questions, evaluate sources (for example websites), and read deeply and critically.	
Decision making skills: I can decide my position on a topic and plan the structure of assignments to demonstrate this position.	

> **Learning tip** If you look back to the assessment criteria in Chapter 10 you will see that 'the ability to self-evaluate' is one feature necessary if a student's work is to get the highest grades. Indeed sometimes students are asked to indicate what they think are the strengths and weaknesses of their work, and to explain the mark they expect, when they hand assignments in.

Approach 1: Discourse communities and academic texts

You saw in Chapter 1 that universities have a culture, in any country the universities will share an understanding of expected ways for teachers and students to behave, and they will have assumptions about what knowledge is and how it should be created and communicated. One result of this is that universities can be thought of as **discourse communities,** meaning they share understandings of the features which a text should have if it is to be considered a true academic text. This general university culture has within it smaller subcultures, for example different subject areas will give greater or lesser value to the different types of primary research you looked at in Chapter 8. In particular, in some subjects qualitative research is seen as equal in value to quantitative research, while in other areas it has no value at all. Also the structuring of a journal research article which you saw in Chapter 9 will vary depending on subject area. The subjective style of writing used to demonstrate reflective learning is acceptable in some forms of texts, but in other texts (and in other subject areas) only objective writing is acceptable. So as well as entering the general discourse community of the university you are also entering the specific discourse community of your subject: psychology, education, management and so on.

> **Learning tip** This is another reason to read widely, for as well as learning the main concepts of your subject, and the subject specific language, you are also learning about the types of texts used; the structure and style of language which is expected, accepted and respected in that field.

You saw in Chapter 6 that a student of economics is joining a discussion which is at least 200 years old, while someone studying CSR is entering a debate which is certainly more than 50 years old. A student therefore needs to demonstrate that s/he has read extensively and has a good idea of the topics which have been raised over the years in this ongoing discussion in this discourse community. These ideas will be included again and again in later writings, and the key concepts will be quoted repeatedly.

Think of a human pyramid in a circus: at the base of the pyramid are the original thinkers in any subject area, above them the later thinkers, at the very top is you – the new student 'standing on the shoulders of giants'. This phrase is believed to have been first used over 300 years ago by Sir Isaac Newton, the scientist who wrote in 1676, 'If I have seen further it is by standing on the shoulders of Giants', thus the voice of this great thinker is brought into this text by referring to his ideas.

A key feature of academic writing, then, is that texts always refer to earlier texts and ideas, and this creates a dilemma for students. You are being pulled in two directions:

- On the one hand, you are not allowed to just give your opinions about a topic. We know that everybody has opinions and believe that one purpose of discussion is to force us to examine and adapt our opinions in order to explain and justify them. However, every point you make in an assignment must be supported by research.
- On the other hand, you cannot just copy out the ideas you find in your research and use them in your own assignment unless you follow the rules of citation and referencing which you will examine in this chapter.

To complete the process of producing assignments you started in Chapter 9 this chapter will examine how to avoid the biggest danger which can come from this dilemma: being accused of plagiarism, and the Skills section will then look at referencing and final editing skills.

Learning tip   Although some students do set out to cheat, plagiarism probably happens more often when a student is under too much pressure, which is why we have looked repeatedly at time management. If you feel under pressure then you need to ask yourself if you have got a good balance between studying and other things in your life. Remember the sources of support in universities mentioned in Chapter 1; if you begin to worry, you should get support from these services.

Method 1: Avoiding plagiarism

You have repeatedly seen the importance of referencing (or citation) in this book, and shown that you should use references to demonstrate the research you have done while still producing something which is in your own voice. This will show you are critical and evaluative; the highest levels of learning. Plagiarism is claiming that something is yours when in fact you are taking the words of other people. Plagiarism can have serious consequences, for example lower marks, failure, even expulsion from the university. This can happen when students know they are cheating and consciously copy something from elsewhere (from a book, an article or another student's essay) and then submit this as if it is their own work, but it can also happen when a student is not sure of what is expected. This chapter aims to clarify what plagiarism is and how to avoid it.

Learning tip Your university will certainly have a clear policy concerning plagiarism, which will explain what is acceptable and what is not acceptable. This will probably be given to you during your induction programme and will be available on the university intranet. Make sure you read this guidance carefully.

Task 11.2   Small group discussions

Discuss these five situations: what do you think about the student's behaviour in each?

1   It is near the end of term and there are several assignments to complete, so the student gets a friend to help by writing one part of an assignment.
2   The student copies out a section directly from a book, and gives a reference, but changes only a few words so decides not use quotation marks.
3   The student copies sections from an essay written by a student who did the same course last year.
4   The student buys an essay from an online site.
5   The student pays someone who has better English to re-write an assignment.

Now read these comments on the five situations:

1   *This is not acceptable*: you are encouraged to discuss your work with other students, but getting other people to do your work is cheating.
2   *This is not acceptable*: it is a mistake to think that making minor changes transforms someone else's words into your own. To be acceptable you need to 'put away' the original text then explain what the key ideas were. Quotations should only be small extracts, not complete sections. Also check back to the idea of critical reading in the previous chapter: you must report on the text you are referring to but you must also give your evaluation and judgement of it.

3   *This is not acceptable* and will not succeed, as most universities these days expect that you will submit your assignment online so they can then get an authenticity report (see the Learning tip below), which will compare your assignment to previous ones.

4   *This is cheating* and will not succeed, as the authenticity report will show where it was taken from.

5   *This is not acceptable*: but you should take advantage of the official support provided by the university which will help you to improve your own English level.

Learning tip   One of the sites most commonly used by universities in connection with this is Turnitin. This site has a lot of information and student guides connected to producing assignments which will satisfy university requirements. Visit the site at: http://turnitin.com/static/index.html

---

Task 11.3   Reading

Look again at the student's summary of Maslow's hierarchy you first read in Chapter 1. Remember, however, that this is just a short summary, it is not intended to demonstrate a complete students' assignment. Notice in particular how the writer gives citations to his or her sources.

Task 11.4   Pair work

Now answer these questions about the summary:

- How many texts does the student refer to in the summary?
- How many times does the student give a reference to each of these sources?
- Are there any direct quotations from the source texts?
- Does the student only give a citation when she uses direct quotations?

Learning tip   Look at these two examples from the summary:

1 This is important for managers because they must understand what motivates the workers in their organization: 'True motivation is achieved by fulfilling higher order needs' (Times100 2005).

2 In order to demonstrate Maslow's theory in its most simple way, Santrock (2004) points out that if students are hungry they are unlikely to be able to do their best.

Example 1 uses a direct quotation, and this is shown by quotation marks, whereas example 2 paraphrases an idea taken from Santock – however both examples use citations to clearly point to where the ideas came from.

Task 11.5 Pair work

In this short extract Baker (2003: 6) is describing the 'Product life cycle'.

> Thus at birth or first introduction to the market a new product initially makes slow progress as people have to be made aware of its existence and only the bold and innovative will seek to try it as a substitute for the established product which the new one is seeking to improve on or displace. Clearly, there will be a strong relationship between how much better the new product is, and how easy it is for users to accept this and the speed at which it will be taken up. But, as a generalization, progress is slow.

Now look at these four different ways a student has tried to incorporate Baker's ideas, discuss each one before you look at the learning tips below; for each one discuss if the student's work is acceptable.

1   According to Baker (2003) at the first introduction to the market a new product initially makes slow progress as people have to be made aware of its existence and only the bold and innovative will seek to try it as a substitute for the established product which the new one is seeking to improve on or displace. So there will be a strong relationship between how much better the new product is, and how easy it is for users to accept this and the speed at which it will be taken up.

2   According to Baker (2003) 'Thus at birth or first introduction to the market a new product initially makes slow progress as people have to be made aware of its existence and only the bold and innovative will seek to try it as a substitute for the established product which the new one is seeking to improve on or displace. Clearly, there will be a strong relationship between how much better the new product is, and how easy it is for users to accept this and the speed at which it will be taken up'.

3   A concept often used is 'Product life cycle'. According to Baker (2003) new products are slow to introduce and only a few people will try it, to see if it is better than other ones. Clearly, there will be a strong relationship between how much better the new product is, and how easy it is for users to accept this and the speed at which it will be taken up.

4   A concept often used is 'Product life cycle'. According to Baker (2003) new products are slow to introduce and only a few people will try it, to see if it is better than other ones. Baker says 'Clearly, there will be a strong relationship between how much better the

new product is, and how easy it is for users to accept this and the speed at which it will be taken up'.

Learning tip

(1) *Unacceptable*. Although the student has given a reference the paragraph is almost entirely Baker's words (there are just two changes). There are no quotation marks.

(2) *Unacceptable*. Although the student has given a reference the paragraph is entirely Baker's words, and even though there are quotation marks this is really too long to be a quotation; it does not show that the student has understood, or evaluated the idea at all. Quotations should also have page numbers.

(3) *Unacceptable*. Although the student has given a reference one sentence is entirely Baker's words, and there are no quotation marks.

(4) *This is better*: it gives the reference and it uses quotation marks for the section which uses Baker's words, but remember quotations should also have page numbers. Be careful not to have too many quotations. This section will be much better if the student then adds research from another source, if the student gives real-world examples, and evaluates the usefulness of the concept of PLC.

Skill 1: Referencing

The assignment instructions you saw for the branding and charities report in Chapter 9 clearly stated that the report must use Harvard referencing and include a bibliography, and you will find that the grading criteria for most assignments will allocate some marks for correct referencing and presentation of work. The biggest mistake is to think of referencing as being a tiresome task to make your life as a student difficult; on the contrary, when you begin any assignment you should set out to try to include as many references as possible, in order to demonstrate that you are an autonomous learner and have read extensively, and you should also aim to do the referencing perfectly to demonstrate that you are now a member of the university discourse community and know the appropriate ways of behaving.

> **Learning tip**   There are a large number of referencing systems, and it is even possible that while you are studying you will need to use a different system for different modules. Here you will look at the general principles and demonstrate these by using the Harvard system. If you need to use a different system there should be guides given by your university, and also there are many clear and simple guides on the Internet.

It is a mistake to try to rush doing the referencing. When you finish an assignment you must spend a lot of time checking that you have correctly identified quotations as being quotations, that when you have paraphrased information you have changed the words but kept the meaning, and that you have followed the rules of citation and referencing. Things cannot be 'almost right' when it comes to referencing, everything must be completely right.

What do teachers say?

Course leader in research methods:

> In the first instance we use references to show what we have read, that we have understood the key ideas of the main thinkers and also the most recent applications or examples of these ideas. But it is more than that. We need to show that we have understood what we have read – this is why a paraphrase or summary, that is re-writing the ideas in our own words, is a much better sign of learning than a quotation. Copying something out does not demonstrate understanding; a photocopier does not understand what it is reproducing! The assignment is intended to show that you have gone through the higher learning processes, analysis, synthesis, and evaluation. References are used to analyse an idea, to apply it to a particular problem, to support or contrast it with other ideas from other sources, to build up our own argument.

Task 11.6   Pair work

Discuss these common misunderstandings about referencing: try to correct them before you look at the Learning tip below.

1   It is enough just to list the sources you have read in your reference list / bibliography.
2   You should only give references when you use direct quotations.
3   You only need to reference each book or article once.

Learning tip

(1) *Wrong!* Referencing has two sides to it: the way you refer to it in the text (surname and year) and the complete details in the bibliography at the end.

(2) *Wrong!* You give references for ideas, even when re-written in your own words.

(3) *Wrong!* You give a reference each time you bring in an idea from any writer you may need to reference one book several times even in one paragraph.

Task 11.7   Name and date

Now check back to the example summary concerning Maslow's hierarchy in Chapter 1, and look specifically how the student used citations inside the summary.

- For one text the student has both the family name of the author and the year it was published: (Santock 2004). This is what you should try to do if at all possible, do not use the authors given names, or initials, or the title of the book or article. If you are uncertain which of an author's names is the family name then you should ask someone.
- For another text the student has not been able to find the name of the specific author, so instead has given the 'corporate author' and the year it was published: (Times100 2005).
- For the third text the student has not been able to find the year the article was published, so gives the corporate author and 'n.d.' meaning 'no date': (Wirral Metropolitan College n.d.).

Task 11.8   Online readings

You should first do some online research to find on the Internet two readings concerning strategic management, a topic which involves thinking about an organization's long term aims and then devising plans and organizing resources so that the organization can succeed. Look for one text using the key words 'Porter five forces', and one text using 'SWOT analysis'. Both of these are extremely famous models and you will find thousands of hits, so practise the skills of evaluating sources you looked at in Chapter 9 to decide if the source you choose is reliable, up to date, and written by someone who can really claim to be an expert.

Then on the website connected to this book www.openup.co.uk/internationalstudents read an example of a student's essay concerning 'management strategy'. Read through it quickly; it is not being used as an example of a perfect assignment, as it is neither particularly good nor particularly bad. As you read it notice how the student makes references both in the essay and in the reference list at the end.

Learning tip   You will sometimes find the list of sources at the end of a text called 'Bibliography' and sometimes 'References' and in some texts there will be both. What is the difference? In general 'References' refer to the sources which this text has specifically taken ideas from, that is they have been referenced (or cited) in the text. A 'Bibliography' is a longer list of all works connected to the topic, including sources not referred to in this text. Students should follow the directions given in their assessment guides; normally you should only list those sources you have referred to and can call this list either 'References' or 'Bibliography' depending on whichever the course guide uses.

Task 11.9   Formatting the bibliography/reference list

Look at these ways of listing the most common types of sources. Notice that the details are very specific, so look carefully at:

- The different uses of punctuation (stops, commas, colons).
- The different uses of fonts (plain, bold, italic).
- The different shapes of brackets.

Books

Bowman, C. and Asch, D. (1987) *Strategic Management*. Basingstoke: MacMillan Press.
Danesi, M. (2006) *Brands*. Abingdon: Taylor & Francis Inc.

Chapters in edited books

De Chernatony, L. (2003) Brand building, in M. J. Baker (ed.), *The Marketing Book*, 5th edn. Oxford: Butterworth-Heinemann.

Journal articles

Soars, B. (2003) What every retailer should know about the way into the shopper's head, *International Journal of Retail & Distribution Management*, 31(12): 628–37.

Websites

Kurtzman, J. (1998) *An Interview with Chris Argyris: Stratgegy and Business.* [online]. New York: Strategy & Business. Available at: http://www.strategy-business.com/press/article/?art=14746&pg=0 (accessed 21 April 2008).

Times100 (2005) *Motivation* [online]. Tadcaster: MBA Publishing Ltd. Available at: http://www.thetimes100.co.uk/downloads/theory/motivation.pdf (accessed 21 April 2008).

Online journals

McArthur, D. N. and Griffin, T. (1997) A marketing management view of integrated marketing communications, *Journal of Advertising Research* [online], 37(5): 19. Available at: http://web3.searchbank.com/infotrac/session/66/850/10267118w3/15!xrn_12&bkm (accessed 1 March 1998).

Now discuss these questions

1. For a book, what order must you put these in: date of publication, title, family name of author, publishing company, author's initials?
2. How do you separate family name from initial?
3. How do you write two authors names down?
4. How do you reference a chapter written by one person included in a book edited by another person?
5. What is the difference between where you put the initial of an author and where you put the initial of an editor?
6. What does 5th edn mean and why is it there?
7. How is the use of italics in the reference for an article different from the use of italics in the reference for a book?
8. What are the differences between referencing websites and online journals?
9. When are (round brackets) used and when are [square brackets] used?

Learning tip The best tip is this: referencing is complicated, so don't try to learn all these complex rules. Instead follow a referencing guide, either supplied by your university or download one from the web, but make sure you are using the correct system of referencing for each assignment you do.

What do students say?

English student of history:

> You must reference very carefully and very accurately! I'm a history student and it's very important to reference everything you say and everything you put down. Because you have to be very careful not to get involved in any kind of plagiarism at all so you really need to look very carefully into what it is you are writing.

Chinese student of Marketing:

> I also find that referencing is very important. I think it is important for students to have a referencing guide with them when you are actually doing assignments. That's what I do. I normally have a referencing guide to hand when I do my assignment and follow the requirements of the referencing guide. Even commas and capital letters are important. I also found a time saving method; to do your referencing while you're doing your assignment rather than to leave it to the last day when you try to do all the referencing together because it takes a much longer time than you think.

Learning tip   From the beginning of your course you should keep your own ongoing reference list, properly arranged from the beginning, which you will build up during your degree course.

Incorporating quotations in your work

Introducing quotations can be a challenge. The obvious way is to use 'says/ said' but you cannot use these all the time. There are a number of other verbs which you could use instead. As you do your own extensive reading learn the verbs that are often used to incorporate ideas, but notice that they have differences in meanings and the strength of the claims to knowledge they are introducing;

- *Discovered, found out*: these are used to talk about the findings of research.
- *Suggested, argued, speculated*: these are used to introduce a theory which is not proven.

Task 11.10

Look at these verbs and check with a dictionary that you understand their uses:

maintain; imply; infer; suggest; indicate; prove; diagnose; attack; reject; look at; argue; describe; conclude; explain; think; report.

Skill 2: Checking

You have now come to almost the final stage of the process of preparing an assignment, but the difference between an average mark and a good mark often depends on what you do now. It is important to think of two distinct phases when writing:

- **Phase 1:** when you are being creative, when you are focusing on the ideas.
- **Phase 2:** after you have incorporated the ideas into the essay, when you go repeatedly through the essay to edit it. This relates to time management, you should plan to finish your assignment and leave enough time to go through it several times in order to polish the language. It is not possible to get a high mark if you do not do this.

If you just hand in your assignment as soon as it is finished your mark will be low. Before you hand it in there are still more steps in the process. Look at the following checklist:

- Leave it for a couple of days, then read it with a fresh eye; ask yourself if you have really discussed the question correctly and addressed the correct aspect of the question (not a similar question or a similar aspect).
- Have you followed the instructions about length, etc.?
- Does the assignment have a clear structure (remember you looked at this earlier), do the sections follow on well from each other?
- Have you read a range of different authors and a range of different types of texts?
- Have you clearly shown which ideas come from your research and which ideas are yours. (Have you clearly shown that you do have ideas and are not just reporting on other research?)
- Have you included examples of applications of these ideas, recent statistics and case studies?
- Have you synthesized these ideas (definitions, statistics and examples) by showing how they connect to each other, how they build up your argument?
- Is the information you have used correct, and correctly referenced?
- Check the English – do not try to write beautiful literature, just clear, simple sentences.

Task 11.11   Portfolio task

You have now almost finished this book. The last portfolio activity is to write a reflective essay to describe your thoughts and feelings about everything you have found out about the culture of learning described here. Put this in Part A of your portfolio.

Remember these points:

- Use the first person pronoun as subject: *I, my, we, our.*
- Use verbs which focus on your thoughts, feelings or actions: *believe, know, feel, think, understand, mean, recommend.*
- Use personalized expressions: *it seems to me, it appears, from my point of view, in my view, in my opinion, as far as I can tell/see.*
- Use verb forms which show how you value things: *should, must, ought to, will, can, shall.*
- Use signals of opinions like: *certainly, definitely, undoubtedly, unquestionably, clearly, obviously, fortunately, unfortunately, unhappily.*

Employability link

Although you may think that you will not need a CV (in America these are often called a 'Résumés') until you graduate, you should in fact begin to prepare one now. The advice from the careers advisor in Chapter 1 included saying that the careers service helps students to prepare their CVs. One of the main reasons for doing this early on is that it will help you to identify gaps – in experience or skills – when you still have the time to fill them before you graduate. For example an international student at one university in the UK started to organize a team in a local six-a-side football league: he was able to use this in his CV to demonstrate not just team working skills but also organizational skills.

Task 11.12   Create your CV

Follow this example to record your own skills and experiences, and if you have little to add about skills and experience start to think how you can fill these gaps:

Name: Ahmed Yahia
Address: 18 Main Street, Anytown, UK.
Phone: 04545534678
Email: a.yh3345@myuniverity.ac.uk
Personal profile:

- Postgraduate student in marketing, with experience in retailing and service industries in the UK, looking for further opportunities to develop skills in related industries.
- Keen to develop existing skills and experience in cross-cultural management situations.

Skills:
 Languages

- Bilingual in Arabic and English.

Strong interpersonal communication

- Previous work placement experience in supermarket to deal with internal and external phone calls and other retailing requirements.
- Negotiation with academic and industrial supervisors in order to be successful in the placement.

Effective communication and presentation skills, both business and academic situations.

- Presented aspects of international students acculturation for new students during induction courses.
- Presented marketing campaign pitch in a national marketing agency.

Team working skills developed both in educational settings and work experience

- Contributed in many academic group projects.
- Highly involved as a team player in work placement.
- Contributed great value in organising and running sporting events.

IT skills

- Competent with range of Microsoft Office applications and Adobe Photoshop.
- Highly competent in a range of business computing applications such as stock control and price control systems in the retail business.

Cross-cultural awareness, having worked in multicultural situations

- Demonstrated by successful adaptation to living, studying and working in a new culture and country from the age of 18.

Full UK driving licence

Education:
2007–Present: University of Anytown, UK
MA Marketing
    Modules studied included: International Marketing Strategy; Scenario Marketing; Strategic Digital Marketing, Research Methods.
2003–2007: University of Anytown, UK
BA (Hons) Advertising with Design
    Modules studied included: Brand Management; Campaign Planning; Issues in Advertising and Design; Integrated Marketing Planning.

1998–2007: General High School, Hometown, Certificate of General High School Graduation.
Modules studied include: Arabic; English; Physics; Geography; Mathematics.
Work experience:
October 2002–Present: Cityfresh Supermarket Ltd.

- Currently working in the administration office to deal with price, advertising and cash issues.
- Working in other departments previously, such as stock control and customer relations.
- Range of skills have been developed, such as communications, customer service awareness, team working.

Interests and activities:
Music, travelling, many sports.

Task 11.13   Critical incident discussion

Critical incidents are descriptions of situations where something has gone wrong, and from them it is possible to glimpse how inappropriate behaviours have resulted from cultural differences. Read through the following critical incident then discuss the questions below.

Try to find more than one possible or acceptable answer to each question: the aim is not to find a 'correct' answer, but to see that different explanations are possible for any situation.

Everybody liked the twins as soon as they arrived at the university: they always studied together in the way they had done throughout their schooling back home. They shared a room on campus and studied the same modules, so they always sat together but had a lot of other friends. For their first assignment in a module concerning retailing they had to do a review of the supermarket sector in the UK and illustrate it with a particular case study of one chosen supermarket. Together they found a lot of material, including up to date analyses of the sector, newspaper reports, customer satisfaction surveys and so on. They then worked together to write a report and, still working together, produced two different case studies of two different supermarkets, one for twin A and one for twin B. The authenticity reports which their tutor received showed that over 70 percent of their reports were the same, the only differences being the case studies. When the tutor asked to see the twins they quite happily explained exactly what they had done, and that this is the way they had studied since the age of 5.

- Can you think of some positive aspects of what the twins did?
- Can you think of some negative aspects of what the twins did?
- Do you think this is plagiarism?
- What do you think the tutor should do?

References

Baker, M. J. (ed.) (2003). One more time – what is marketing? *The Marketing Book*, 5th edn. Oxford: Butterworth-Heinemann.

Glossary

Note this glossary explains the meanings of the words as they are used in this book, in other contexts many of the words will have different meanings.

Analysis: one of the higher levels of learning, analysis means to be able to take something apart (for example a problem, a theory, a case study) to see how different parts of it are connected.

Applications of theory: a common requirement of many assessments is that students can illustrate a theory with a real-world example, in particular that they can use theory to address a real problem.

Assessment criteria: this is the general policy of marking within a university, so that, for example, a B+ in different subjects reflects a similar level of achievement.

Assessments: these are the tasks students do in order to get a mark, there are many different forms of assessment.

Assignments: these are any task that students are given to do. These may or may not be assessments, but you are expected to do them all to engage with the learning process.

Autonomous: this is the idea of working without supervision, for example to find extra readings connected to your course, to choose your own examples (often real-world examples) to illustrate the topics you are studying.

Blog: this is an online diary which can be shared with other people, for example others in a seminar group. These can be used as a form of assessment.

Campus: some universities are in a large park where there are many different buildings including teaching blocks, Halls of Residence, restaurants and shops

Careers service: this is the part of the student services department of a university which helps students to prepare for and find work.

Case studies: these are descriptions of a real example (perhaps an individual person, perhaps a company or organization) which you use as an example of a topic you are studying. You may need to analyse the example, to make recommendations in order to demonstrate that you can apply the theories you have learnt.

Comprehension: in Bloom's taxonomy, this refers to a low level of learning of just demonstrating understanding. Note that in many other uses 'comprehension' is not connected with low levels of learning.

Constructivist: this is describing a theory from psychology that each person creates their own understanding of the world based on their own experiences, and – in social constructivism – they do this by interacting and discussing with other people.

Continuous assessment: this is an approach to assessment where tasks are given at different stages throughout a course.

Copy and paste: students' work which consists largely of extracts they have taken from several sources and which does not demonstrate high levels such as synthesis and evaluation.

Credits: different components of a course may earn the student a number of credits (for example perhaps one module is worth 20 credits) and you need to collect a fixed number of credits to pass your course.

Critical awareness: this is a recognition that all claims to knowledge (for example ideas presented in books) can be questioned, hence learning is not primarily about remembering but more about the higher order behaviours like analysis, synthesis and evaluation.

Critical incidents: this is a technique used to develop cross-cultural understanding, where a situation is described in which the participants have a culturally different understanding of what the rules are. Discussion of the situation helps students to appreciate differences.

Culture shock: this is an experience that people may have when they first enter another culture, where they may find differences can cause stress and anxiety.

CV: this stands for curriculum vitae. It is a summary of skills, experiences and qualifications used to apply for jobs.

Declarative knowledge: this is the ability to state something which is known. This is often not seen as a high level of learning.

Degree: this is an award given to a student who has successfully passed a university course at a certain level.

Discourse communities: these are groups of people who share a common way of using language and making texts, for example lawyers or social workers, who will have their own styles of speaking and writing.

Discourse markers: these are words or phrases used to show a connection between two ideas: *for example, on the other hand* and so on.

Discussion boards: these are Internet facilities where a group of people can hold a discussion by posting questions and responses.

Dissertation: this is an extended student assignment, often involving primary research, which can be the final step in getting a degree.

Distance learning: this is a course where students do not physically attend the university but use post or Internet to receive information and complete assignments. These are sometimes supported by short sessions where groups of students and teachers do meet face to face.

End of course assessment: this is used in contrast to continuous assessment, often based on examinations but can include many types of assignment, such as summative portfolios.

e-Portfolios: this is a version of portfolios where students use online methods of creating and keeping their learning portfolios, either for study of for CPD.

Ethnography: a method of research in many areas such as business organizations, health care, criminology and education. Ethnographers try to understand how people in a culture (such as the culture inside a company or inside a university) identify themselves and their roles.

Evaluation: this is often seen as the highest of all levels of learning. It involves not just repeating, analysing and synthesizing information but also the ability to make a judgement about it (for example the worth, the uses, the suitability in certain situations).

Exchange: this involves schemes where students go to another country for a part of their course and transfer the credits they achieve back to their original university.

Extensive: this is a term used in contrast to 'intensive'; an initial stage of study where you focus on getting a broad and general understanding, by reading a large number of texts quite rapidly.

Faculty: this is a specific academic part or department of a university, for example the Faculty of Health or the Faculty of History.

Feedback: this is any kind of comment, written or spoken, which a student gets about assignments and performance, from teachers or from other students, which is then used to feed forward to improve future work.

Field trip: this is when a group of students, for example in geography, go out of the university in order to collect samples which they will later analyse and report.

Figures: these are diagrams, drawings or pictures which help to show the connection of ideas like an image, used to convey complex information clearly.

Formative assessment: this refers to methods used to find out how students are progressing during a course, not included in course final grades.

Freshers' week: new students are sometimes called freshers, and at the beginning of the university year there is often a week when the different clubs, societies, sports team and so on explain what they do and try to attract new members.

Functional knowledge: this is the ability to use knowledge in order to do something, for example to solve a specific problem.

Glossary: this is a list of definitions of how words are used in a specific topic area; for example the definition of 'demand' in a glossary of economics will be more specific than a definition in a general dictionary.

Grades: when work is assessed it is given a mark or grade. There are several methods of doing this, some courses will have marks like B+ or C−; others will use percentages; others will have broad categories like Pass, Merit and Distinction.

Group work: this is when students work together, perhaps to complete some form of project, intended to develop the skills of working with other people, requiring a range of management, interpersonal and communication skills.

Hall of residence: this is a building, sometimes on campus and sometimes in city centres, where a large number of students live, usually in single or double rooms. Some are self-catering, others have meals at set times.

Harvard referencing system: this is just one of many ways to show the sources of ideas used in a piece of writing. These systems are complex and must be applied correctly.

Individual learning plan: this is a description of skills and knowledge a learner needs and a step by step description of how these will be achieved.

Induction: this is a period (perhaps one or two weeks) when new students are introduced to the different parts of the university, when you make choices about your modules, and you learn about facilities like student service and the IT department.

Information and communication technology (ICT): key skills often include the ability to use a variety of computer skills: word processing packages; saving and organizing your own files; working with email; searching for information on the Internet; using software such as PowerPoint to give presentations; using spreadsheets to process numerical information; making graphs.

Informed consent: when carrying out primary research it is usually necessary to explain to any participants what the research is aiming to do and getting them to agree to be involved, for example before interviewing.

Intended learning outcomes: these are explanations of what students should know and be able to do as a result of studying a particular course.

Intensive: this is a term used in contrast to 'extensive'; the stage of focused thinking and reading necessary to satisfy the specific requirements of an assignment.

International foundation programmes: these are usually one-year courses for international students to prepare them for studying at university.

Interpersonal skills: these are the skills necessary to get on with other people in team work, or when dealing with clients and customers, including skills like active listening and communication.

Interpretivism: this is connected to research which is concerned with obtaining each person's view of a situation. Usually connected with qualitative research methods.

Interview schedule: this is the list of topics which a researcher will get a participant to talk about in a semi-structured interview.

Key skills: these link what students study to their future employability; the skills that people need in any employment regardless of their specific job or profession: communication; application of number; information technology; working with others; improving own learning and performance; problem solving.

Knowledge: in Bloom's taxonomy this refers to a low level of learning of just remembering and repeating information. Note that in many other uses 'knowledge' is not connected with low levels of learning.

Lectures: these are where large numbers of students listen while the lecturer discusses the many theories in that subject area, to show how they are connected, for example how some key thinkers developed the ideas of earlier thinkers or how one school of thought differs from another.

Likert scale: this is used in many questionnaires to give a numerical ranking to attitudes, for example strongly agree can be +2, and strongly disagree can be −2.

Literature review: this is a type of assessment or part of an assessment based on critically reading a large number of texts on a related topic, showing connections between them.

Module: in some university courses students study a series of specific modules each covering different aspects of the subject.

Module and course guides: these are overall descriptions of courses given to students at the outset, containing intended learning outcomes, a guide to assessments, an indicative reading list and any other general course information.

Objective: this is a style of writing where the focus is on the topic being discussed with no direct reference to the thoughts and feelings of the writer, hence s/he uses impersonal forms such as the passive voice. Used in contrast to 'subjective'.

Online groups: these are where students use the Internet for collaborative work, such as supporting research projects. They are also suitable for distance learning where participants cannot meet in the real world. These often make use of social networking facilities such as blogs and wikis.

Open-book exams: these are when you can take in some books and notes to refer to during the exam.

Paraphrases: these are ideas taken from reading and rewritten using the students' own words, around the same length as the original.

Peer assessment: this is where students give each other marks, particularly used in seminar tasks such as presentations; this is intended to make students more aware of how assignments are assessed.

Peer reviewed: this is the process where books and research articles are examined by other academics before they are published to check on the quality of scholarship.

Personal development portfolio (PDP): this is used in many professions to collect evidence of skills and competences developed throughout a career, so it records your personal journey through life and is evidence to refer to in job applications. The PDP it is never complete, as these things are always open to change.

Plagiarism: this is presenting other people's words and ideas as if they were your own, this can include copying from other students or from sources such as books and the Internet.

Portfolio: this is a collection of examples, reflections, exercises and other kinds of evidence of learning which is built up over a period of time. A method of reflective learning which can be used for assessments and for PDP.

Positivism: this is connected to research which is concerned with obtaining careful and accurate measurement of things in the world (weights, volumes, temperatures and so on, hence it uses quantitative methods) in order to understand scientific laws – 'hard facts' – and to understand causes and results.

Postgraduate: this is advanced study after getting the first degree, for example Masters' or doctorate.

Pre-departure courses: these are courses run for groups of students before they leave their home country: they deal with topics like culture shock, study skills and English language competence.

Presentation: this can be used generally to describe the appearance of students' work, for example you make sure that reports have a professional presentation, but it is used more specifically to describe an oral presentation where a student (or a group of students) need to describe and discuss a topic or project to a group of people as a form of assessment.

Primary research: this is to carry out an investigation in order to gather new information (data), for example connected to a group project or an individual dissertation. Common techniques include interviewing, using questionnaires, observing situations and carrying out experiments.

Project: projects often are carried out by groups, and demand extensive work over a period of weeks or even months to investigate some question or problem. After doing this research the group must report their findings sometimes both as an oral presentation and as a written report.

Qualitative: this involves research methods which collect people's words, for example when you interview participants or ask them to keep a diary which you will analyse.

Quantitative: this involves research methods which collect numerical data which you can then analyse statistically.

Reading for gist: this is quick, general reading to get a general idea of the topic of a text.

References: these are the sources of information which you have used in order to complete any form of assignment. Referencing is also called citation.

Reflective learning: this is an approach to learning where you to think about experiences in order to amend future actions.

Reports: these – unlike essays – are arranged with clear section headings, and when used as student assessments are often based on various professional formats: a title page; a contents page; an executive summary; theoretical background; the case study; your findings from primary research; your recommendations.

Research methods: these are the ways of collecting information (data) in order to better understand a situation. Some are qualitative and some, quantitative.

Role playing: this is a method of learning by acting situations used in some forms of training or seminars, for example acting out how to deal with angry customers or how to interview candidates for jobs.

Scanning: this is a method of quick reading which involves looking through a document in order to find a specific piece of information, for example looking for one specific name in a list of names.

Secondary research: this is using already published data which you find and then do a new analysis of, for example analysing a company's stock market valuations for a period of time.

Self-assessment: this is where students give their own work a mark intended to make students more aware of how assignments are assessed and so will keep on target.

Seminars: these are learning activities which usually involve quite small groups of students participating in discussions, for example of case studies, linked to the idea that knowledge is socially constructed.

Skimming: this is a method of quick reading which involves looking over a document very rapidly just to get a general idea of what it is about and how it is organized.

SMART objectives: these are used in an approach to setting objectives which can be used for making plans; the objectives should be specific, measurable, attainable, relevant, time-bound.

Social construction: this is a theory from psychology that each person's understanding of the world is based on experiences, and by interacting and discussing with other people.

Socratic education: this is a phrase used to describe the theory behind seminar discussions; the teacher creates a dialogue by asking questions which set off discussions, rather than questions looking for a single answer which is 'correct'.

Student led seminars: these are seminars which are organized by students, sometimes working in groups, to introduce and discuss a topic, can be a type of assessment.

Students' union: in just about every university there is a students' union which is run by and for students, concerned with general aspects of students' lives and providing social opportunities.

Subjective: this is a style of writing where the focus is on the thoughts and feelings of the writer, for example related to reflective learning, hence uses personal forms such as 'I think that . . .' Used in contrast to 'objective'.

Summaries: these are ideas taken from reading and rewritten in a shorter form using the students' own words.

Summative assessment: this is any way of finally giving students marks, most crucially passing or failing a module or course.

Support services: these are the departments in a university which exist to help students in areas like accommodation, health and careers. Often they are the first place to go if you are unsure about anything at all.

Surveying: this is a method of quick reading where you do not look at every word of a text or article. For example you may read only the introduction and then the first sentence of each of the other paragraphs.

Synthesis: this is a high level of learning where something new is created by combining other ideas, examples, findings and so on in a new and original way.

Taxonomy: this is a scheme of classification, for example grouping the natural world of plants and animals.

Time constrained test: this is a type of assessment where students are allowed to think about a topic before finally answering it in normal examination conditions

Top-up: this is a type of course where students add to an existing qualification (for example to convert a diploma into a degree) by doing part of the higher course. A common example is a 2 + 2 course.

Transferable skills: see key skills.

Transmission model: this is a theory of learning which assumes that knowledge is like a thing that can be given by one person to another: teachers know a lot, students know little, therefore teachers should transmit knowledge to students.

Undergraduate: this is the first degree students study at university, the most common being BA (Bachelors of Arts, and BSc (Bachelor of Science). These can be honours degrees, for example BA (Hons), or ordinary degrees.

VAK (visual, auditory and kinaesthetic) model: this is one of many models concerning learning styles, suggesting that some people mainly learn by seeing, some by listening, and some by touching.

Virtual learning environments (VLEs): many modules now are supported by virtual learning environments, which are on a university's intranet. Tutors use these to communicate with students, to post activities and case studies for you to read, or to link you to course readings. These VLEs can also have discussion boards where student can exchange ideas, for example when they are doing group work. Many lecturers will post their PowerPoint slides from lectures on the VLE.

Volunteering: this is doing unpaid work for example helping with charities, working with the elderly or children – a way of getting richer life experiences.

Work placement: this is spending a period of time working in a situation related to your studies, as well as getting real-life experience you may need to complete some assignments (for example a work related project) in order to earn credits. These may be as short as a month or as long as a year.

Index

THE COMPLETE GUIDE TO REFERENCING AND AVOIDING PLAGIARISM

Colin Neville

- Why is there so much emphasis on citing sources in some written work?
- How can I be sure I am referencing sources correctly?
- What is plagiarism and how do I avoid it?

There is a great deal of emphasis on accurate referencing in written work for university students, and those writing for professional purposes, but little information on the 'when', the 'why', as well as the 'how' of referencing. This book fills that gap, giving clear guidelines on how to correctly cite from external sources, what constitutes plagiarism, and how it can be avoided.

A unique feature of the book is the comparisons it makes between different referencing styles – such as Harvard, APA, MLA and Numerical referencing styles – which are shown side-by-side. This provides a useful guide, for students as they progress through higher education, and particularly for those on combined studies courses – who may be expected to use two, and sometimes three, different referencing styles.

Other special features in the book include:

- Essays demonstrating referencing in action
- Exercises on when to reference, and on what is, and what is not, plagiarism
- A 'Frequently Asked Questions' section on the referencing issues that most often puzzle people
- A detailed guide to referencing electronic sources, and advice on how to choose reliable Internet sites

A Complete Guide to Referencing and Avoiding Plagiarism is essential reading for all students and professionals who need to use referencing to accurately reflect the work of others and avoid plagiarism.

Contents
Preface – Acknowledgements – Referencing – Why reference? – What, when and how to reference – Plagiarism – Referencing styles – Harvard style of referencing – American Psychological Association (APA) and Modern Languages Association (MLA) referencing styles – Numerical referencing styles – Frequently asked questions – Referencing in action: example references – Index.

2007 240pp

ISBN-13: 978 0 335 22089 2   (ISBN-10: 0 335 22089 4) Paperback

ISBN-13: 978 0 335 22090 8   (ISBN-10: 0 335 22090 8) Hardback